FABLES: STORYBOOK LOVE

FABLES: STORYBOOK LOVE

DC Comics, 1700 Broadway, New York, NY 10019
A Warner Bros. Entertainment Company.
Printed in Canada. Tenth Printing. ISBN: 978-1-4012-0256-9.
Cover illustration by James Jean.

This volume of love, lust, obsession, revenge, regret and betrayal is respectfully dedicated to Becky, Mary, Amy and Monica, for all of the usual reasons.
— Bill Willingham

Library of Congress Cataloging-in-Publication Data

Willingham, Bill.
Fables. Vol. 3, Storybook love / Bill Willingham, Mark Buckingham, Lan Medina, Bryan Talbot, Linda Medley, Steve Leialoha, Craig Hamilton.
p. cm.
"Originally published in single magazine form as Fables 11-18."
ISBN 978-1-4012-0256-9 (alk. paper)
1. Legends–Adaptations–Comic books, strips, etc. 2. Graphic novels. I. Buckingham, Mark. II. Medina, Lan. III. Talbot, Bryan. IV. Medley, Linda. V. Leialoha, Steve. VI. Hamilton, Craig, 1964- VII. Title. VIII. Title: Storybook love.
PN6727.W52F384 2012
741.5'973–dc23

2012038959

FABLES: STORYBOOK LOVE

FABLES CREATED BY BILL WILLINGHAM

Bill Willingham
writer

Mark Buckingham
Lan Medina
Bryan Talbot
Linda Medley
pencillers

Steve Leialoha
Craig Hamilton
Bryan Talbot
Linda Medley
inkers

Daniel Vozzo colorist
Todd Klein letterer

James Jean
Aron Wiesenfeld
original series covers

WHO'S WHO IN FABLETOWN

KING COLE

A merry old soul and the current elected mayor of Fabletown.

SNOW WHITE

The resourceful deputy mayor of Fabletown — the one who really runs things. She was Prince Charming's first wife. They divorced when she caught him sleeping with her sister.

PRINCE CHARMING

A dashing rogue, incapable of romantic fidelity. He mourns his lost fortunes and lives off the women he seduces.

ROSE RED

Snow White's fraternal twin sister, estranged from Snow for many centuries.

BIGBY WOLF

The Big Bad Wolf of old, who's since reformed and can now assume human form. He's the sheriff of Fabletown.

THE STORY SO FAR

In Book One of FABLES (LEGENDS IN EXILE) we find that...

... Rose Red is missing and presumed dead. In the process of unraveling the mystery, Bigby Wolf leads us on a tour of Fabletown — a secret New York City community populated by the immortal refugees from many magical worlds and kingdoms. These "Fables," as they call themselves, were forced to flee their homelands when the armies of a terrible creature, known only as The Adversary, invaded and conquered them. Eventually Bigby discovers that Rose Red is still alive. Her fabricated murder was a scheme cooked up by Rose and her boyfriend, Jack, to escape their bad debts and her promised betrothal to the dangerous, jealous, and revenge-minded Bluebeard.

BRIAR ROSE

The sleeping beauty of old. Prince Charming's second wife.

BOY BLUE

Snow White's assistant.

BLUEBEARD

The richest man in Fabletown, who claims to have reformed from his old evil ways.

GOLDILOCKS

All grown up, but still living with the Three Bears. She's since become a gun-toting revolutionary.

FLYCATCHER

The frog prince, who can't get over his taste for flies.

JACK HORNER

A schemer and trickster, ever since his beanstalk climbing days. He's perpetually unable to anticipate the long-term consequences of his actions.

This is followed by Book Two of FABLES (ANIMAL FARM) in which...

... Snow White and Rose Red take a trip to the upstate New York Fabletown annex known as The Farm, where those refugee Fables who can't pass as human are forced to live. The sisters arrive just in time to discover a revolution under way — the animal Fables hate being confined to The Farm. Led by Goldilocks, the Three Bears, and the Three Little Pigs, they plan to take over first The Farm and then Fabletown. Then they intend to invade and win back their old homelands, using modern weapons to overthrow the Adversary. With the help of a few loyal animal Fables, Snow White succeeds in stopping the revolution, but not before she is gunned down by an enraged Goldilocks. Miraculously, Snow survives wounds that would have killed any human, possibly because of the magical power conferred on her by her vast popularity among those so-called "Mundys." While Snow convalesces over the course of the next year, the revolutionary leaders (with the exception of Goldilocks, who eludes capture) are tried for their various crimes. Some are executed and others are sentenced to years of hard labor. Rose Red takes over management of The Farm, and Goldilocks remains at large — public enemy number one among the Fables.

Cover art by Aron Wiesenfeld

NOW MAYBE THIS STORY IS TRUE AND MAYBE IT AIN'T, BUT IT'S ABOUT CRAFTY OLD JACK OF THE TALES, WHO WAS A TRICKY FELLOW IN THE OLD WORLD AND CONTINUED TO BE SO WHEN HE FOLLOWED US OVER TO THIS COUNTRY.
The American JACK TALES
WHEN THE WAR OF YANKEE AGGRESSION BROKE OUT--WHICH THOSE OF LOW EDUCATION CONTINUE TO CALL THE AMERICAN CIVIL WAR--JACK, ALWAYS A RESTLESS SORT, GOT IT IN HIS MIND THAT HE COULD TAKE ADVANTAGE OF SUCH A GRAND ADVENTURE.
HE THOUGHT HE MIGHT BE ABLE TO MARRY HIMSELF A RICH SOUTHERN BELLE, IF ONLY HE EARNED SOME RENOWN IN BATTLE.
SO, PUTTING ON GENTLEMAN'S AIRS AND A REFINED MANNER OF SPEECH, JACK CAME DOWN SOUTH AND LIED UP A MESS OF IMAGINARY ESTATES AND ARISTOCRATIC RELATIONS, SO AS TO LIST WITH THE LOUISIANA VOLUNTEERS AS A CAPTAIN OF INFANTRY.

WELL, JACK NEVER GOT HIS GLORY, BECAUSE THE WAR DIDN'T TURN OUT ALL THAT GOOD--AT LEAST NOT FOR THE SOUTHERN GENTRY.

BAG O' BONES
In which death itself proves to be just another occasion for Jack to hatch his schemes.
Written by BILL WILLINGHAM
Illustrated by BRYAN TALBOT
Lettered by TODD KLEIN
Colored & Separated By DANIEL VOZZO
Cover art by ARON WIESENFELD
Assistant Editor: MARIAH HUEHNER
Editor: SHELLY BOND
FABLES created by Bill Willingham
This story was freely adapted from a couple of the Mountain Jack Tales of American folklore. In true oral tradition, it's been much altered under my care, which is a polite way of saying that I stole everything I thought I could use, changed a bunch of stuff to suit my whims, and made up the rest. — Bill

WHEN IT WAS CLEAR TO JACK THAT THE SOUTH WAS LOST, HE LIED SOME MORE ABOUT A DYING MOTHER IN ORDER TO BE GRANTED EARLY MUSTER.
GET OUT, YOU SCURRILOUS IMPOSTOR.
I EXPECT HIS BOSS COLONEL WAS MORE OF A MIND TO LET JACK GO BECAUSE HE WAS A DEFT HAND WITH A DECK OF CARDS, AND THE COLONEL WAS TIRED OF ALWAYS LOSING HIS WAGES TO HIM.
YOU-UNS ALL TAKE CARE Y'SELF NOW.
TAKE THE ROAD, JACK. IT'S LONGER BUT SAFER.
DON'T CUT THROUGH YONDER SWAMP, BECAUSE IT'S WITCHED WITH ALL MANNER OF VILE CRITTER. MEBBE NICK SLICK HISSELF.
SHITFIRE, BOY, I AIN'T A-FEARD OF NO HAINTS.

MAYBE IT WAS TRUE THAT HE WASN'T AFRAID, OR MAYBE HE AVOIDED THE ROAD BECAUSE IT WAS EVEN MORE DANGEROUS. ALL MANNER OF CUTTHROAT BANDS, RENEGADE DESERTERS AND NE'ER-DO-WELLS ROAMED THE CRUMBLING SOUTH IN THOSE DAYS. WHATEVER THE REASON, JACK DID CUT ACROSS THE BAYOU.
WE LOVED EACH OTHER THEN, LORENA, MORE THAN WE E'ER DARED TO TELL...
WELL I'LL BE A SUCK-EGG MULE.
WHAT'S AN OLD COOT LIKE YOU-UNS DOING ALL ALONE AWAYS OUT HERE IN THE MIDDLE A' THE SWAMP?
PLAYING POKER ALL WITH MESELF, TO TAKE MY MIND OFF MY EMPTY BELLY.
SET Y'SELF DOWN A SPELL, YOUNG FELLER, AND PLAY A FEW HANDS WITH ME, SO MEBBE I CAN WIN ME SOME OF THEM TASTY VITTLES OFF YOU.
WELL, I SURELY LIKE A BIT OF POKER, BUT IT DON'T LOOK TO ME LIKE YOU-UNS GOT NARY A THING TO BET WITH.
WHO KNOWS? MEBBE I'M THE KING A' OL' SIAM AND GOT ME ALL SORTS OF TREASURE STASHED AWAY IN MY SACK HERE. YOU JESS BET WHAT YOU'VE A MIND TO AN' I'LL MATCH IT UP.
WELL, I GUESS THAT'LL HAVE TO DO. DEAL THE CARDS.
YOUR BET, YOUNG FELLA.
I RECKON I'LL OPEN WITH A MESS O' CRUSTY, FRESH-BAKED BREAD.
I BET YOU SURE WANT TO WIN THAT, HUH?

THIS IS ONE GAME OF CARDS THAT DIDN'T TURN OUT SO WELL FOR OUR BOY JACK. THE SKINNY OLD SWAMP RAT HAD HIM A RUN OF CARDS LIKE OLD KING DAVID HAD HIM A RUN OF WIVES. THEY WAS ALL LOVELY AND THEY CAME BY THE BUSHEL.
YOUR BET AGAIN.
I KNOW! I **KNOW** IT IS! YOU DON' GOTTA KEEP **TELLIN'** ME TIME AND AGAIN. I'M BETTIN' MY LAST **BOOT** 'GAINST GETTIN' TH' OTHER ONE BACK.
AND THIS TIME I **GOTS** YA, YEZ OL' RIVER PIRATE, 'CAUSE I GOTS A FULL HOUSE, KINGS FULL OF TREYS.
DEM'S GOOD CARDS FOR SURE, BOY, BUT I 'SPECT FOUR LITTLE TWOS IS STILL JESS A MITE BETTER.
DANG IT! YEZ DONE CLEANED ME **OUT**, Y'OL BUZZARD!
YOU DON' WANT TA PLAY NO MORE?
HOW? AH YAINT GOT DOODLY-SQUAT CEPPIN MY **PANTS**, AND I AIN'T ABOUT TO GO CREEPIN' THROUGH THE SWAMP BUCK-ASS **NEKKID!**
THAS NOT **EVERY-THING** YOU GOT, BOY. YOU STILL GOTS YOUR **SOUL**.
HOW 'BOUT IF WE PLAY ONE LASS HAND? YOUR SOUL 'GAINST EVERYTHING I HAVE HERE, MY STUFF AND YOUR STUFF COMBINED.
SO THASS WHAT THIS IS ALL ABOUT. I SHOULD'A RECOGNIZED YOU RIGHT OFF, MR. SLICK.
WHERE'S YOUR HORNS AND TAIL AND CLOVED **HOOFS?**

STICK TO THE SUBJECK. IS WE GON HAVE ONE MORE HAND?
MY DEAL, NICK. EVEN IFFEN YOU WIN THIS TIME, YEZ GIT NOTHIN' BUT USED TRASH.
BUT IFFEN I WIN, AH'M TAKIN' EVERYTHIN' YEZ GOT, LIKE YOU-UNS PROMISED.
EVEN THAT MAGICAL BAG YEZ STUFFED ALL INTO.
OH YEAH, NICKY, I FIGURED THAT MUCH OUT BY MY OWN SELF. I SEEN YOU STUFFIN' MORE AND MORE INTO YONDER SACK, BUT IT DIN'T GET NO FULLER.
HOW MANY CARDS YOU TAKIN'?
I THINK I'LL STICK WITH THESE, THANK YEZ ALL THE SAME.
WELL, MY TWO-DRAW FILLED IN MY ACE-HIGH FLUSH.
BUT THAT DON' BEAT FOUR OF ONE KIND, LIKE YOU SHOWED ME LASS HAND, OLD NICK.
FOUR JACKS.
DANG IT! YOU TRICKED ME SOMEHOW!
NONSENSE. WHO COULD TRICK THE DEBBIL HIMSELF?
SO HOW DOES THIS WORK?

OLD NICK NEVER DID FIGURE OUT HOW HE WAS OUTFOXED. SOME SAY JACK WAS JUST A BETTER CHEATER.
CAMPTOWN RACETRACK FIVE MILES LONG--
OH DA DO DAH DAY!
JACK WAS KNOWN TO BOAST, AT TIMES, WHEN HE WAS DEEP INTO HIS CUPS, THAT HE NEVER DID PICK UP A DECK OF CARDS WHERE HE COULDN'T DEAL HIMSELF ALL FOUR JACKS, WHENEVER HE LIKED.
GLORY BE!
SAY WHAT YOU WILL ABOUT OLD NICK SLICK-- HE NEVER WENT BACK ON NO BARGAIN, ONCE MADE. HE TOLD JACK THE MAGIC WORDS THAT WOULD MAKE ANYTHING GO INTO THE BAG, WHICH WOULD NEVER GET FILLED UP.
HERE, PIGGY-PIGGY!
CLICKETY CLACK! GET INTO MY SACK!
WHOOOOOOOOOSH!
Y'ALL ARE GOING TO MAKE ME ONE FINE AND FANCY SUPPER, MRS. PIGGY.

AN' MAYBE I'LL GET LUCKY TWICE AND FIND ME SOMEONE HERE TO COOK Y'UP FOR ME.
HELLO!
GALLANT HERO OF THE WARS HERE! ANYONE HOME?
ANYONE OWN THESE NICE FAT CHICKENS?
THEN Y'ALL WON'T MIND NONE IFFEN I HELP MESELF TO A FEW.
HERE, CHICKY-CHICKY!
CLICKETY CLACK! GET INTO MY SACK!
HELLO?

JACK SEARCHED THE MANSION HIGH AND LOW, LOOKING FOR ANYONE WHO MIGHT BE THERE TO MAKE HIM WELCOME, AND COOK UP HIS DINNER FOR HIM.
AIN'T NOBODY HERE AT ALL?
WITH ALL THE ROBBERS AND BRIGANDS ROAMING ABOUT, IT WAS DEEPLY ODD TO FIND A RICH ESTATE--EVEN ONE AS RUN-DOWN AS THIS-- LEFT ALL ALONE.
SHOULD I JESS MAKE MESELF AT HOME THEN?
UNTIL HE LOOKED IN THE LAST CORNER BEDROOM OF THE WESTERN WING.
HELLO?
OH MY.
HELLO, SIR. WELCOME TO SARAMORE, MY FAMILY'S ANCESTRAL HOME.
I'M SALLY CORNWELLES.
UH... I'M JACK. I'M A--
DECORATED HERO OF THE WAR? YES, I KNOW. I HEARD YOU FROM THE MOMENT OF YOUR RATHER BOISTEROUS ARRIVAL.

THEN WHY DIN'T YOU-UNS ANSWER NOTHIN'?
A YOUNG LADY OF GOOD BREEDING DOESN'T SCREAM OUT HER GREETINGS LIKE SOME UNEDUCATED HOOLIGAN.

THEN WHY DIN'T YOU COME OUT TO WELCOME ME PROPER THEN?
BECAUSE A DEBILITATING SICK-NESS HAS COME OVER ME, AND I AM QUITE UNABLE TO MOVE FROM MY BED.

YOUAH SICK?
DON'T FRET. IT'S NOT CONTAGIOUS. AT LEAST IT'S ONLY EVER AFFECTED MEMBERS OF MY FAMILY BEFORE.
WHEREAH THEY? YOUAH FAMILY?
ALL GONE NOW, VICTIMS OF THE SAME MORTAL AFFLICTION. I'M THE LAST OF THE CORNWELLES LINE.

NO GENTLEMAN WOULD HAVE ME, KNOWING THAT MY CONDITION WOULD DETERI-ORATE UNTIL I WAS LEFT LIKE THIS.
WE HAVE THE REPUTATION OF BEING CURSED. I'M SURPRISED YOU WERE BRAVE ENOUGH TO VENTURE ONTO OUR LANDS. WE'RE RUMORED TO BE HAUNTED, DON'T YOU KNOW?

AN' THE SLAVES?
ALL RUN OFF OR SOLD LONG AGO. MY NAN STAYED WITH ME, OF COURSE. BRAVE AND LOYAL NAN. BUT WITH DEATH ONLY HOURS AWAY NOW, I SET HER FREE THIS MORNING.

YOU-UNS DOOMED TO DIE?
WITHIN AN HOUR OR TWO. BEFORE NIGHTFALL MOST LIKELY. I'M RESIGNED TO IT NOW. THE LAST OF THE PAIN WENT AWAY DAYS AGO.
THASS HORRIBLE NEWS. YOU-UNS THE MOST LOVELY WOMAN I EVER DID SEE.
YOU'RE VERY COMPLIMENTARY, SIR.
YEZ SHOULDN'T HAVE TO DIE BE-FOAH YEZ EVER DID LIVE.
WE CAN'T CHOOSE OUR OWN FATE.
HEY! I DON'T SUPPOSE YEZ WANT TO HAVE A LAST TUMBLE FIRST? BEFORE THE REAPER COMES TO TAKE YOU?
I AIN'T HAD A WOMAN IN THREE YEARS -- NOT COUNTING WHORES OF COURSE -- AND SINCE YEZ DON' HAVE NO PLANS FOAH THE AFTAHNOON...
EXCUSE ME?
ARE YOU SUGGESTING I INDULGE IN CARNAL CONGRESS WITH YOU? I INTEND TO GO VIRTUOUS TO MY LORD! YOU'RE NO GENTLE-MAN, SIR!
AND LET ME ALSO POINT OUT THAT YOU'RE OBVIOUSLY NO SOUTHERN MAN, EITHER. YOUR COUNTERFEIT ACCENT COMES AND GOES MORE FREQUENTLY THAN A MARCH BREEZE.
OH...YEAH. I GUESS I GOT SO USED TO APING THE SPEECH OF YOU PEOPLE DOWN HERE, I FORGOT TO DROP IT ONCE I LEFT THE INFANTRY. AND WHAT DO YOU MEAN, "COUNTER-FEIT"?

I'LL HAVE YOU KNOW THAT SEVERAL LADIES OF NEW ORLEANS SOCIETY FOUND ME QUITE AUTHENTIC AND CHARMING.
AS AN AMUSING SIDESHOW, NO DOUBT. PLEASE BE GOOD ENOUGH TO LEAVE ME TO MY APPOINTMENT WITH THE DARK ANGEL.

HEY, THAT'S AN IDEA!
WHAT WOULD YOU SAY IF I COULD KEEP OLD RATTLE BONES FROM CLAIMING YOU?

NO ONE HAS THAT POWER. YOU'RE A CRUEL MAN TO EVEN ATTEMPT TO RAISE MY HOPES FOR YOUR SICK AMUSE-MENT.
NO, I'M SERIOUS. DO YOU WANT TO LIVE? WHAT PRIZE WOULD YOU PAY TO ESCAPE DEATH TODAY?
ANYTHING, OF COURSE, BUT--
DEAL!
SIT TIGHT, SALLY, AND LET ME DO EVERYTHING. AND AFTERWARDS, REMEMBER OUR DEAL. I HAVEN'T HAD A WOMAN IN A LONG TIME, AND NEVER ONE AS PRETTY AS YOU.

AH HA, MISTER RATTLE BONES! I'VE GOT YOU NOW!
EH?
CLICKETY CLACK! GET INTO MY SACK!
WHOOOOOSH!
YOU DID IT, JACK! YOU CAPTURED DEATH HIMSELF!
AND, HEY--I CAN MOVE AGAIN. THE PARALYSIS IS GONE!
HOW DO YOU FEEL, GIRL?
PERFECT. WONDERFUL.
ONCE MORE, I AM THE HERO OF THE DAY. AND NOW TO CLAIM MY HERO'S REWARD.
YYYYUUUGGHH!
I KNOW WHAT I HAVE TO DO, AND I WON'T GO BACK ON MY BARGAIN, BUT--
--IS THERE ANY POSSIBILITY YOU'D BE WILLING TO BATHE FIRST?
ANYTHING FOR YOU, MY SWEET.

OH DEAR GOD ABOVE, THIS IS A FILTHY THING YOU'RE MAKING ME DO.
FILTHY!
I FEEL SO DIRTY!
AM I DIRTY, JACK? AM I?
I AM DIRTY, AREN'T I, JACK?
CALL ME A DIRTY GIRL, JACK!
CALL ME A DIRTY GIRL!
DO IT! CALL ME A STRUMPET! A WHORE!
I'M SO BAD! I'M SO DIRTY!
JESUS GOD ABOVE, SALLY!
CAN'T YOU JUST SHUT UP FOR A MOMENT? LONG ENOUGH TO LET ME FINISH?
I'M GOING TO BUST OPEN JUST TRYING TO KEEP UP WITH YOU, WOMAN!

OH, JACK, WHAT A GLORIOUS WORLD YOU'VE OPENED UP FOR ME.
HOW LONG BEFORE YOU CAN GO AGAIN?
YOU'RE KILLING ME. I NEED TO SLEEP.
IF YOU'VE STILL GOT SO MUCH ENERGY LEFT, GO COOK MY DINNER--OR IS IT BREAKFAST NOW?
GO SLAUGHTER SOMETHING. I'LL NEED A LOT TO REPLENISH EVERYTHING YOU'VE TAKEN OUT OF ME. GO ON.
QUIT PUSHING ME. I'M GOING.
WAKE ME WHEN IT'S READY.
PIG.
OR BEEF OR CHICKEN.
I'M NOT PICKY, AS LONG AS THERE'S LOTS OF IT.
COME HERE, YOU!

GOT YOU!
SQUAAAWK!
SETTLE DOWN, GIRL, IT WILL ONLY HURT A MOMENT.
SQUAWK!
SQUAWK! SQUAWK! SQUAWK!
SQUAWK! SQUAWK! SQUAAAWK!
EEEYAH!
WHAT WITCHERY IS THIS?

JACK?

JACK?

WAKE UP, JACK!

SALLY!
WHAT HAPPENED?
NOTHING WILL DIE, JACK.
COME SEE. COME SEE FOR YOURSELF.

HOLD ON. QUIT PULLING ON ME, YOU DOTTY WENCH!

SEE WHAT I MEAN, DARLING?
OH MY.
MOOAAA!
RHEEEE!
SNOOORT!
SQUAWK!
SQUAWK!
SQUAWK!
SQUAWK!
MOOOO!
SQUAWK!
SQUAWK!
SNOOORK!

SQUAWK!
SQUAWK!
SQUAWK!
SQUAWK!
SQUAWK!
SQUAWK!
SQUAWK!
SQUAWK!

WHAT HAVE I DONE?
AND THAT'S NOT ALL, MY LOVE. WE HAVE VISITORS.
AND I THINK THEY'RE HERE TO SEE YOU.
JACK.
JAAAACK.
WHAT HAVE YOU DONE, JACK?
WE WERE KILLED IN THE BATTLE THIS MORNING, JACK, BUT WE CAN'T DIE.
WHY HAVE YOU KEPT US FROM GOING TO OUR REWARD?
WHAT HAVE YOU DONE?

THIS ISN'T MY FAULT, BOYS. NOT REALLY. I JUST WANTED TO SAVE THE GIRL.
LOOK AT HER. WOULDN'T YOU WANT TO KEEP HER OUT OF OLD RATTLE BONES' CLUTCHES, IF YOU COULD?
DON'T PUT THIS ON ME, JACK. I WAS READY TO GO TO MY SWEET SAVIOR'S BOSOM.
YOU'VE DESTROYED THE WAY OF THINGS, JACK.
WAIT! I THINK I CAN STILL PUT IT RIGHT.
WAIT HERE! DON'T MOVE!
I CAN FIX THIS.
ALL I NEED TO DO IS--
COME OUT OF THERE, MISTER BONES.
HURRY, JACK, MORE THINGS ARE ARRIVING.
HORRIBLE THINGS.
WHOOOSH!
HOW DID YOU DO THAT TO ME?
NOW, DON'T GET ANGRY, SIR. I CAN EXPLAIN EVERYTHING.

ANGRY? WHY WOULD I BE ANGRY?
THAT WAS THE FIRST DAY OFF I'VE EVER HAD. IT WAS WONDERFUL! I FEEL SO RESTED!

THEN EVERYTHING'S OKAY BETWEEN US?
AS LONG AS YOU LET ME TAKE A DAY OFF IN YOUR MAGIC BAG ONCE EVERY YEAR OR SO. NOW, IF YOU'LL EXCUSE ME, I HAVE SOME WORK TO CATCH UP ON.
BUT WHAT ABOUT ME? AM I TO BE TAKEN NOW TOO?

I'LL GIVE YOU ANOTHER YEAR TOGETHER. THAT'S THE BEST I CAN DO.

ONE YEAR, REMEMBER.
AND OH WHAT A LOVELY YEAR IT WILL BE! WON'T WE BE HAPPY, JACK MY LOVE?
UH... SURE, SWEETHEART. IT WILL BE GRAND. BUT ONLY--

YES, MY DARLING?
COULD YOU TAKE A BATH FIRST?
BUT JACK LOST BOTH HIS SWEETHEART AND THE MAGIC BAG WITHIN A FEW WEEKS OF THAT DAY. LOVELY SALLY RAN OFF WITH A TRAVELING PREACHER AND WHISKEY DRUMMER. AND THE BAG? WELL, MAYBE THAT'S A TALE BEST LEFT FOR ANOTHER TIME.
NEXT: A TWO-PART CAPER

Cover art by James Jean

HERE'S A NASTY LITTLE WINTER'S TALE...
THIS IS SERIOUS, BRIAR ROSE.

YOU FELL ASLEEP AGAIN, IN THE MIDDLE OF TIFFANY'S.

I COULDN'T HELP IT, BIGBY.
I PRICKED MY FINGER ON A DIAMOND PIN AT THE JEWELRY COUNTER.
CAUSING THE ENTIRE SALES FLOOR TO FALL ASLEEP WITH YOU?

A Sharp Operation
Part One of a Two-part Caper
Written by Bill Willingham
Pencilled by Lan Medina
Inked by Craig Hamilton
Lettered by Todd Klein
Colored and Separated by Daniel Vozzo
Cover art by James Jean
Assistant Editor Mariah Huehner
Editor Shelly Bond
FABLES is created by Bill Willingham
CUSTOMERS AND CLERKS ALIKE?

UNFORTUNATELY THAT'S THE WAY THE OLD ENCHANTMENT WORKS. FIRST I PRICK MY FINGER ON SOMETHING AND FALL ASLEEP. THEN EVERYONE AROUND ME FALLS ASLEEP, AND THEN THE THORN FOREST STARTS GROWING AROUND WHATEVER BUILDING I HAPPEN TO BE IN.

WE GOT LUCKY THIS TIME. THEY THINK SOME KIND OF GAS LEAK CAUSED IT. BUT WE CAN'T HAVE INCIDENTS LIKE THIS. NOT OUT AMONG THE BLOODY MUNDYS.
I DON'T THINK THE ENCHANTMENT CARES WHERE I AM, OR AMONGST WHOM.
F.B.I.
WANTED
DEC

I THOUGHT IT WAS ENDED FOR ALL TIME BACK IN THE HOMELANDS, WHEN PRINCE CHARMING KISSED ME -- BUT APPARENTLY ALL THAT DOES IS RESET THE SPELL TO ITS STARTING POSITION.
IT'S AN ENDLESS CYCLE.

THEN YOU'RE JUST GOING TO HAVE TO STOP PRICKING YOUR FINGERS. YOU'RE STILL WEALTHY ENOUGH. GET SOME WORKMEN TO GO THROUGH YOUR APARTMENT AND REMOVE ALL THE ROUGH EDGES AND SHARP CORNERS.
AND WHEN YOU GO OUT, WEAR GLOVES. THICK ONES.

THAT MIGHT WORK WHILE WINTER LASTS, BUT NOT WHEN SPRING COMES.

BIGBY?
EVEN THEN. RICH PEOPLE ARE SUPPOSED TO HAVE ECCENTRICITIES. LET THAT BE YOURS.
KNOCK KNOCK

EXCUSE ME FOR INTERRUPTING, SHERIFF, BUT TRUSTY JOHN NEEDS YOU OUTSIDE.
CHRIST ABOVE. WHAT NOW?

IT'S A MUNDY GENTLEMAN LOITERING OUTSIDE THE GATE, SIR.
SO? WE GET MUNDYS PASSING THROUGH FABLE-TOWN ALL THE TIME. THEY DON'T KNOW THIS ISN'T PART OF THEIR CITY.

EXCEPT THAT THIS ONE ASKED FOR YOU BY NAME.

ELSEWHERE IN THE CITY.
I WANT YOU OUT! OUT OF MY APARTMENT AND OUT OF MY LIFE!

I'M ALREADY TWO STEPS AHEAD OF YOU, MOLLY DEAR. WHILE YOU WERE SLEEPING, I SENT MY LUGGAGE INTO STORAGE. IF NOTHING ELSE OVER THE YEARS, I'VE LEARNED TO ANTICIPATE WHEN A ROMANCE HAS RUN ITS NATURAL COURSE.
MOLLY?!
WHO'S MOLLY?!

OOPS. SLIP OF THE TONGUE. I HAVE TO CONFESS, I CAN NEVER RE-MEMBER WHICH PRETTY LITTLE GIRL I'M BUNKING WITH THESE DAYS. WHICH ONE ARE YOU AGAIN? DAPHNE? TRISH?

I KNEW IT! I KNEW YOU WERE SNEAKING OTHER WOMEN IN HERE WHILE I WAS OUT! AND I KNOW YOU'VE BEEN STEAL-ING MONEY FROM ME!
YES, I'M A TERRIBLE CAD.
YOU TAKE CARE NOW, BETTY, OR CHRISSY, OR WHOEVER YOU ARE.

OKAY, PRINCE CHARMING, WHERE TO NOW?

AND BACK IN FABLETOWN...
OKAY, WHAT'S YOUR STORY, FELLA?
MR. WOLF?
THAT DEPENDS. WHO THE HELL ARE YOU AND WHAT DO YOU WANT?

OH, I KNOW IT'S YOU ALL RIGHT. I KNOW ALL ABOUT YOU.
I'M TOMMY SHARP. I WRITE THE SHARP COMMENTS COLUMN FOR THE DAILY NEWS. PERHAPS YOU'VE READ IT?

NOPE. I READ THE POST.
AND YOU'RE ALREADY BEGINNING TO BORE ME. WHY DON'T YOU SAY WHAT YOU WANT TO SAY AND MOVE ALONG?

FINE. THEN HERE'S MY BUSINESS IN A NUTSHELL. FOR THE PAST FEW YEARS I'VE BEEN WORKING ON A STORY ABOUT YOUR UNDERGROUND COMMUNITY.

I'VE PUT IN THE HOURS, CHECKED AND DOUBLE-CHECKED THE RESEARCH AND DONE THE LEG-WORK.
HOW LOVELY FOR YOU.

I KNOW ALL YOUR SECRETS.
THEN YOU'RE WAY AHEAD OF ME.

AND, AS A JOURNALISTIC COURTESY, I'VE DECIDED TO FINALLY REVEAL MYSELF--COME OUT OF THE SHADOWS, SO TO SPEAK--
--IN ORDER TO GIVE YOU AN OPPORTUNITY TO RESPOND, BEFORE I PRINT MY STORY.
RESPOND TO WHAT? SO FAR YOU'VE ONLY BABBLED NONSENSE.

TAKE THAT EVASIVE TACK IF YOU LIKE, BUT I KNOW WHAT I KNOW.
GET THAT THING OUT FROM UNDER MY NOSE.
YOU'RE A COMMUNITY OF IMMORTALS--PROBABLY.

IN ANY CASE YOU'VE EACH BEEN ALIVE FOR CENTURIES, TUCKED AWAY IN THIS QUIET LITTLE CORNER OF THE CITY.
YOUR GROUP HAS OWNED EVERYTHING ON THIS BLOCK SINCE BACK WHEN NEW YORK WAS STILL CALLED NEW AMSTERDAM.

I'VE GOT RECORDS. I'VE COMPILED PERSONAL HISTORIES. I'VE DUG UP PICTURES OF A NUMBER OF YOU--DATING BACK TO THE VERY BEGINNINGS OF PHOTOGRAPHIC TECHNOLOGY--AND NOT A ONE OF YOU HAS AGED A DAY.

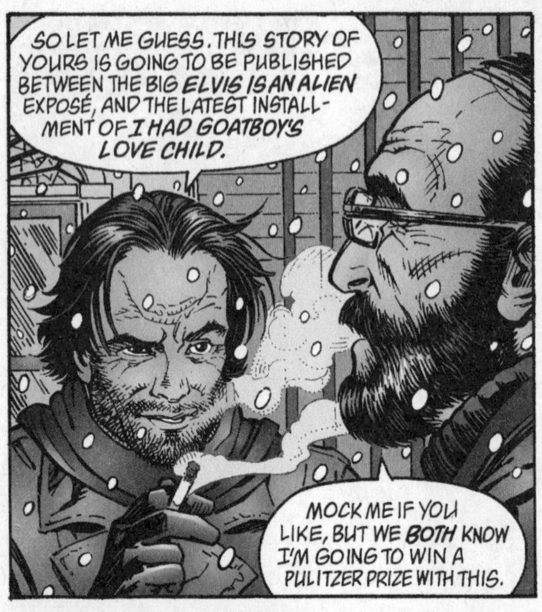
SO LET ME GUESS. THIS STORY OF YOURS IS GOING TO BE PUBLISHED BETWEEN THE BIG ELVIS IS AN ALIEN EXPOSÉ, AND THE LATEST INSTALL-MENT OF I HAD GOATBOY'S LOVE CHILD.
MOCK ME IF YOU LIKE, BUT WE BOTH KNOW I'M GOING TO WIN A PULITZER PRIZE WITH THIS.

MAYBE EVEN THE NOBEL PRIZE--
--FOR BEING THE FIRST TO COME UP WITH UNIMPEACHABLE PROOF OF THE EXISTENCE OF YOUR KIND.
AND JUST WHAT DO YOU IMAGINE "MY KIND" IS?

VAMPIRES OF COURSE.
SERIOUSLY?

OH MY GOD, YOU ARE SERIOUS.
A GROUP OF IMMORTALS, WITH FANTASTIC POWERS, PASSING THEMSELVES OFF AS NORMAL HUMANS? I'VE READ ANNE RICE. I'VE SEEN THE MOVIES. IT ALL FITS.

YOU PROVIDED THE FINAL, CONVINCING PROOF. I FOLLOWED YOU, ON ONE OF YOUR AFTER-HOURS JAUNTS TO CENTRAL PARK. I WATCHED YOU STRIP DOWN, THEN ASSUME ANIMAL FORM, FOR A MIDNIGHT RUN. THAT'S WHAT VAMPIRES CAN DO, RIGHT?

YOU DIDN'T SEE ME, DID YOU? THANKS TO MY TELEPHOTO LENS, I WAS ABLE TO STAY FAR AWAY.
AND YET YOU WERE DUMB ENOUGH TO GET WITHIN EASY REACH OF ME NOW?

ONLY IN THE DAYTIME, WHEN YOU HAVE NO POWER OVER ME. YOU CAN'T MESMERIZE ME NOW. YOU CAN'T HURT ME... uhm... CAN YOU?
YOU'RE INSANE.

PLAY IT THAT WAY, IF YOU INSIST.
BUT YOU DON'T HAVE LONG TO GET YOUR SIDE OF THE STORY ON RECORD BEFORE I PUBLISH.

SHOVE OFF, CLOWN.

HERE'S MY CARD, MISTER WOLF. CALL ME IF YOU CHANGE YOUR MIND.
AND DON'T THINK FOR A MOMENT YOU CAN CATCH UP TO ME AFTER THE SUN GOES DOWN.

I KNOW HOW IT WORKS. I'LL BE SAFELY HOME BY THEN, AND VAMPIRES CAN'T ENTER MY PERSONAL RESI-DENCE WITHOUT MY INVITATION.
I'M NOT AFRAID OF YOU.
I'M REALLY NOT.

LATER THAT SAME DAY.
WE'VE GOT TROUBLE.
IN THE WOODLAND'S RATHER BIZARRE BUSINESS OFFICE.
IF SHARP'S EXPOSÉ IS PUBLISHED, OUR LIFE HERE IS EFFECTIVELY OVER. EVEN IF NO ONE OFFICIAL BELIEVES THE STORY, ENOUGH MUNDY KOOKS AND GOTH-FREAK VAMPIRE WANNA-BES WILL.
SO WHAT'S THE PROBLEM? WE SHOULD KILL THIS GUY--
--JUST LIKE THAT LAST POOR BASTARD WHO FOUND OUT ABOUT US BACK IN THE TWENTIES.
I KNOW HOW TO MAKE IT LOOK LIKE A SUICIDE.
SNOW WHITE
I'VE CONSIDERED THAT, BLUEBEARD. I WISH WE COULD AND I ALMOST DID HIM MYSELF OUT ON THE STREET.
BUT WE'RE IN THE INFORMATION AGE, AND THIS TOMMY SHARP CHARACTER IS TOO WELL KNOWN. EVERY-THING'S INTERCONNECTED NOW. EVEN IF WE KILL HIM IN A WAY NO ONE SUSPECTS AS MURDER, IT'S NO GUAR-ANTEE HIS STORY WON'T COME OUT.

SHOULDN'T MISS WHITE BE HERE?
NO. DESPITE MY PREFERENCES, THIS MAY END UP REQUIRING SOME DIRTY BUSINESS.
AS LONG AS SHE'S STILL CONVALESCING, I WANT SNOW KEPT OUT OF IT.
SNOW
DIRECTOR OF

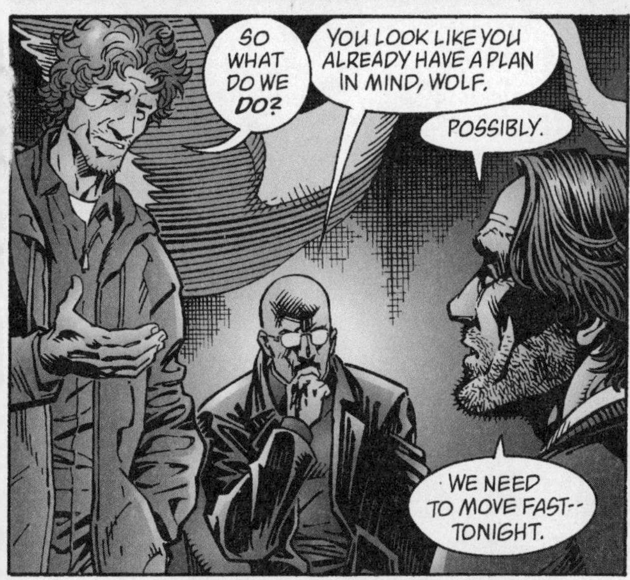
SO WHAT DO WE DO?
YOU LOOK LIKE YOU ALREADY HAVE A PLAN IN MIND, WOLF.
POSSIBLY.
WE NEED TO MOVE FAST-- TONIGHT.

BUT FIRST WE HAVE TO FIND OUT WHERE PRINCE CHARMING IS CAMPING THESE DAYS.
AND WE'LL NEED BRIAR ROSE'S HELP.

SLEEPING BEAUTY? WHY? WHAT DO YOU HAVE IN MIND?
A SCHEME WORTHY OF YOU, JACK, EXCEPT THAT THIS ONE HAS A POSSIBILITY OF SUCCESS. WHEN YOU TRIED YOUR DOT COM SCAM LAST YEAR, JUST HOW GOOD DID YOUR COMPUTER SKILLS GET?

IN BLUEBEARD'S APARTMENT.
I DON'T CARE WHAT THE WOLF HAS IN MIND. WE NEED TO PREPARE FOR A MORE DIRE RESOLUTION TO THIS PROBLEM-- JUST IN CASE.

IF YOUR PERSONAL HISTORY ISN'T ENTIRELY FABRICATED, JACK, YOU'VE UNDERTAKEN DANGEROUS BUSINESS BEFORE. IF THE TALES ARE TO BE BELIEVED, YOU WERE ONCE A GIANT-KILLER OF SOME RENOWN.
YOU'RE NO STRANGER TO THE PRECISE AND WILLFUL APPLICATION OF DEADLY FORCE.
SO WHAT? ALL OF US HAVE VARIED CAREERS IN OUR PAST.

IT'S ONE OF THE BYPRODUCTS OF BEING LONG-LIVED.

THESE WEAPONS ARE CLEAN. UNTRACEABLE. TAKE ONE.
CARRY IT IN AN OUTSIDE POCKET WHERE YOU CAN GET AT IT QUICKLY --TO USE IT OR DISPOSE OF IT, AS NEEDED.

IF WE CAN RESOLVE THIS BIGBY'S WAY, ALL TO THE GOOD. BUT IF THE WOLF'S PLAN FAILS--
--WE NEED TO BE READY TO STEP IN.

PARDON THE INTERRUPTION, SIR.
MISTER WOLF IS READY TO GO.
WE'RE ON OUR WAY.

AND SO...
HEAD DOWNTOWN, TOWARDS TRIBECA. SHARP LIVES IN ONE OF THOSE RITZY APARTMENT BUILD-INGS OFF HUDSON SQUARE.

EVERYONE KNOW THEIR PARTS?

PRINCE CHARMING AND BRIAR ROSE-- YOU'RE UP FIRST.
LET ME HELP YOU, MY DEAR. THIS SNOW MAKES FOR TREACHEROUS FOOTING.
AND YOU WOULD KNOW "TREACHEROUS" WHEN YOU SEE IT, DEAR--

--BEING SO PERSONALLY EXPERIENCED AT IT.
NOW NOW, DARLING, THIS IS NO TIME TO DREDGE UP THE PAST.
REMEMBER: WE'RE A DELIRIOUS-LY HAPPY MUNDY COUPLE.

TWO OF THIS TOWN'S SEEMINGLY ENDLESS SUPPLY OF BUBBLE-HEADED SOCIALITES.
I'LL DO MY PART, "DARLING," BUT KEEP YOUR HANDS TO YOURSELF.

GOOD EVENING, SIR, MA'AM. THIS IS QUITE A SPOT OF WEATHER WE'RE HAVING, EH?
THANK YOU, MY GOOD MAN.
AFTER YOU, HORTENSE, MY DOVE.

YOU'RE NOT RESIDENTS HERE, ARE YOU?
NO, OF COURSE NOT.
WE LIVE SOMEPLACE NICE.

WE'RE HERE FOR THE BIG PARTY.
WHAT PARTY WOULD THAT BE, SIR?
GOOD QUESTION.

WHO ARE WE SEEING TONIGHT, SWEET-HEART?
HOW SHOULD I KNOW?
WHO CAN KEEP TRACK?
WELL, I CAN'T LET YOU GO UP UNTIL I KNOW WHO YOU'RE HERE TO SEE.
I HAVE TO CALL AHEAD. THIS IS A SECURITY RESIDENCE.

I'M GROWING BORED, MORTIMER.
DO SOMETHING.

DASH IT ALL, HONEYBEAR, I MUST HAVE LEFT THE INVITATIONS OUT IN THE COACH.
JUST SIT HERE FOR A MOMENT AND I'LL FETCH THEM.

DRINK UP, BE MERRY, AND I'LL BE BACK IN TWO SHAKES.

SHE'S IN.
GOOD. NOW WE WAIT.
THEN CAN WE WAIT BACK IN THE CAR?
IN CASE YOU HADN'T NOTICED, IT'S WINTER OUT HERE.

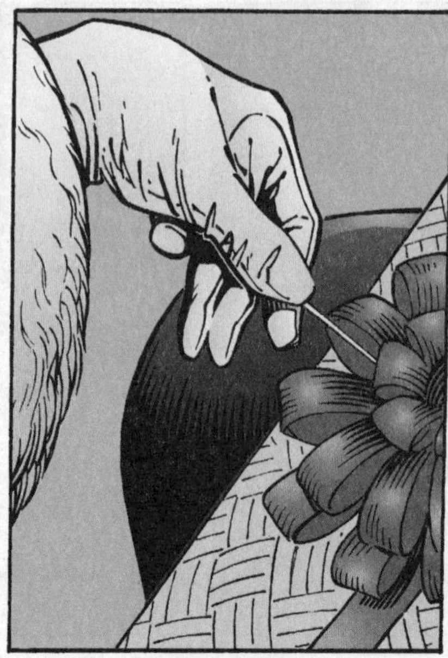

YAWN

YAWN

ZZZZZZZZ
ZZZZZZZZ

WHEN CAN **WE** GO IN?
NOT FOR A WHILE YET.

"BE PATIENT, BOY BLUE."
SNOOOOORE!
POWER GOLD

"WE HAVE TO GIVE BRIAR ROSE'S ENCHANTMENT TIME TO DO ITS WORK.

"AS ITS EFFECT SPREADS OUT, EVERYONE IN THE BUILDING SHOULD FALL ASLEEP.

"EVERY PERSON IN EVERY APARTMENT--
"--ALONG WITH THEIR DOGS, CATS, GERBILS AND PARAKEETS."
HELLO? **BETH?** ARE YOU STILL **THERE?**

I THOUGHT YOU WERE COLD.
BLUEBEARD WON'T LET ME SMOKE IN THE LIMO. CAN I BUM A BUTT OFF OF YOU?
WHEN ARE YOU GOING TO LEARN TO SUPPORT YOUR OWN FILTHY HABITS?
IT'S BEEN ALMOST AN HOUR NOW.
CAN WE GO IN YET?
NO. IF WE GO IN TOO SOON, WE'LL FALL UNDER THE SLEEPING SPELL OURSELVES.
HOW WILL WE KNOW WHEN IT IS SAFE THEN?
WE'LL KNOW BECAUSE I'LL KNOW.
THEN I'LL TELL THE REST OF YOU.
DOES THIS NUTJOB REALLY THINK WE'RE VAMPIRES?

APPARENTLY.
THAT'S KIND OF COOL. IF WE WERE VAMPIRE'S WE'D ALL BE RICH.
HOW SO?
THINK IT THROUGH. VAMPIRES MAKE MORE VAMPIRES JUST BY SUCKING PEOPLE'S BLOOD, RIGHT? DO YOU KNOW HOW MUCH THESE MUNDY FUCKS WOULD PAY TO SOMEONE WHO COULD MAKE THEM IMMORTAL?
HEY! I JUST THOUGHT--!
FORGET IT, JACK.
FORGET WHAT?
YOU JUST REALIZED YOU COULD MAKE USE OF THE SAME OLD PICTURES OF YOURSELF AND THE REST OF US--THAT SHARP FOUND--TO CONVINCE GULLIBLE, RICH MUNDYS THAT YOU ARE A VAMPIRE, AND CHEAT THEM OUT OF THEIR MONEY...
...BY PROMISING TO MAKE THEM IMMORTAL.
HOW--?
I'M WAY AHEAD OF YOU, JACK. I ALWAYS WILL BE.
AFTER ALL THESE YEARS, I KNOW HOW YOUR MIND WORKS. TRY IT AND I'LL LOCK YOU UP FOR A CENTURY.
DAMN IT, BIGBY!
SHUT UP, JACK.
THE THORN-GROWING PHASE HAS STARTED.

IT'S TIME TO GO IN.

SHARP LIVES ON THE SEVENTH FLOOR. JACK AND BOY BLUE ARE WITH ME. BRING THE TOOLS.
FLYCATCHER, YOU AND THE PRINCE FIND THE SECURITY OFFICE.
THE SECURITY CAMERAS' FEED IS BEING RECORDED SOMEWHERE, AND WE'LL WANT TO TAKE THE TAPES WITH US WHEN WE GO.

BLUEBEARD MANS THE DOOR.
FIND THE KEYS AND LOCK IT TIGHT.

NO ONE COMES IN UNTIL WE'RE DONE.

DOES ANYONE ELSE FEEL LIKE WE'RE IN A CAPER FLICK?

THIS IS THE RIGHT DOOR. GET IT OPEN, QUICK.
DON'T MISS.
7D

SMASH!
WOO HOO! WE'RE IN!

JACK, FIND HIS COMPUTER AND GET TO WORK. HE'S PROBABLY USING ONE OF THE BEDROOMS AS AN OFFICE.
BLUE, FIND MISTER SHARP AND MAKE SURE HE'S ASLEEP. THEN HELP ME TOSS THE PLACE. WE NEED TO LOOK AT EVERY PHOTOGRAPH AND DOCUMENT IN HERE.
ROGER DODGER, SHERIFF!
WORK FAST, BUT WORK SMART, TOO. DON'T CUT CORNERS.

AND SING OUT IF YOU START GETTING SLEEPY. WE CAN'T AFFORD TO BE CAUGHT HERE.

LOOK AT YOU, TOMMY.
PLEASE, GOD, LET THERE BE A CAMERA HERE. WE NEED A PICTURE OF THIS.
ZZZZZZZZZZ

I FOUND SHARP, BUT YOU'VE GOT TO COME SEE THIS FOR YOURSELF.
DON'T BOTHER ME, SONNY BOY. I'M WORKING.

TIME CREEPS BY AND THE BUILDING CONTINUES TO SLEEP...
...EXCEPT FOR A HANDFUL OF LATE INTRUDERS.

DID WE GET EVERYTHING PERTAINING TO US?
I THINK SO. HE HAD A COMPLETE DARKROOM FULL OF ALL SORTS OF PICTURES OF US.
I'VE GOT GOOD NEWS AND BAD NEWS, BIGBY.
I SUCCESSFULLY KILLED EVERY FILE HE HAD--NO PROBLEMO, BUT I HAD A LOOK THROUGH HIS E-MAIL RECORDS. HE BACKED UP ALL OF HIS WORK BY SENDING IT OUT.
SHIT. WHAT NOW?

OUT? WHAT DO YOU MEAN OUT? OUT WHERE?

THERE ARE SECURE PLACES ON THE INTERNET YOU CAN SEND STUFF--FILES--ANYTHING YOU WANT TO PROTECT FROM PEOPLE LIKE ME.
IT LOOKS LIKE SHARP MADE FREQUENT USE OF THESE SYSTEMS.

SO WE'VE WASTED ALL THIS EFFORT? WE CAN'T GET TO THOSE DUPLICATE FILES?
NOT WITHOUT PUTTING A BETTER COMPUTER HACKER THAN ME TO WORK FOR A WEEK, OR MORE.
SO SHARP WINS, WE'RE SCREWED.
THAT DEPENDS, I HAVE AN ALTERNATE PLAN. BUT IT DEPENDS ON HOW EVIL YOU'RE PREPARED TO GET.
NEXT: REALLY DIRTY DEEDS.

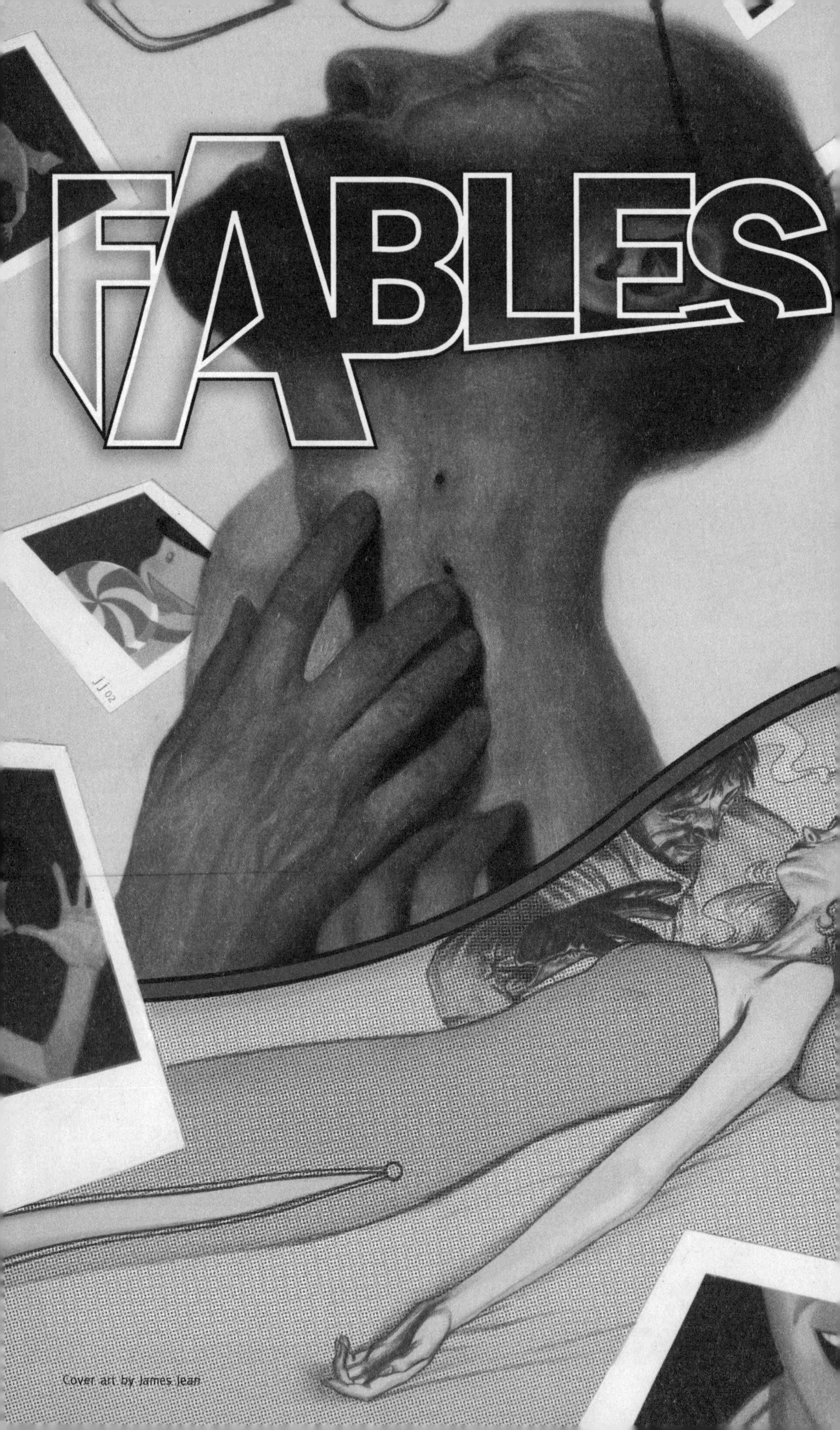

Cover art by James Jean

LOOK AT THIS -- BIGBY WOLF AND HIS INTREPID TEAM OF FABLES ARE IN THE MIDST OF WATERGATING TOMMY SHARP'S APARTMENT...
STEP AWAY FROM THE MAN, BLUEBEARD! AND PUT THAT DAMNED GUN AWAY.
WHY?
SINCE WE CAN'T BE CERTAIN WE'VE DESTROYED ALL OF SHARP'S FILES, WE NEED TO IMPLEMENT A MORE DRASTIC SOLUTION.
SO LET'S KILL HIM AND BE DONE WITH IT.
AREN'T YOU SUPPOSED TO BE DOWNSTAIRS, WATCHING THE DOOR?
Dirty Business
Part Two of a Two-part Caper
Written by Bill Willingham
Pencilled by Lan Medina
Inked by Craig Hamilton
Lettered by Todd Klein
Colored and Separated by Daniel Vozzo
Cover art by James Jean
Assistant Editor Mariah Huehner
Editor Shelly Bond
FABLES is created by Bill Willingham

MAYBE I DIDN'T MAKE MYSELF CLEAR. BACK OFF OR I'LL KILL YOU.

SHOW SOME BACKBONE FOR ONCE, WOLF.
YOUR NON-VIOLENT PLAN DIDN'T WORK, SO NOW WE'RE FORCED TO FALL BACK ON MORE EXTREME, BUT MORE CERTAIN MEASURES.

I'M WILLING TO DO IT, SO YOU DON'T HAVE TO WORRY ABOUT GETTING YOUR OWN PAWS DIRTY.
YOU CAN EVEN LOOK AWAY, IF YOU'RE REALLY SO SQUEAMISH.
MAYBE WE SHOULD GET OUT OF THE WAY.
YES, JACK--

--MAYBE YOU SHOULD.
DON'T BOTHER. SINCE NONE OF YOU HAS THE STOMACH FOR ROUGH BUSINESS, I WON'T FORCE IT.

WE'LL DO IT BIGBY'S WAY-- ASSUMING HE EVEN HAS AN ALTER-NATE PLAN.

ACTUALLY, IT'S MY PLAN.
THEN IT'S SURE TO SUCCEED, JUST LIKE EVERY OTHER SCHEME YOU'VE CONCOCTED OVER THE YEARS.

CUT IT OUT.
WE'VE GOT A LOT OF WORK TO DO AND NOT MUCH TIME IN WHICH TO DO IT.

JACK, YOU AND BOY BLUE GET TOMMY SHARP READY FOR TRAVEL.
BLUEBEARD, GET BACK DOWN TO THE LOBBY, WHERE YOU WERE SUPPOSED TO BE ALL ALONG.
THE ENTIRE POPULATION OF THE CITY COULD BE DOWN THERE BY NOW.
AND I'D STILL BE THERE IF I HAD ANY CONFIDENCE IN YOU.

SO YOU'VE MANAGED TO TELL US, AD NAUSEAM.
WHAT HAPPENED TO YOU SINCE THE EXILE?

WHEN DID THEY TAME YOU?

OR WAS YOUR FORMERLY SAVAGE NATURE ALWAYS COUNTER-FEIT?
A COMBINATION OF BLUSTER AND DEFT PUBLIC RELATIONS?
DARK ROOM

DON'T PUSH THIS ANY FURTHER.
OR YOU'LL RIP MY THROAT OUT, OR KILL ME, OR BLAH BLAH BLAH?
YOU'VE SAID IT ALL BEFORE, WOLF.

YOUR CONSTANT "OR ELSES" HAVE GROWN TEDIOUS.
HASN'T ANYONE TOLD YOU THAT THREATS LOSE THEIR IMPACT WHEN SO OFTEN REPEATED, WITHOUT EVER ACTUALLY ACTING ON ONE OF THEM?

I HAVEN'T NEEDED TO ACT, BECAUSE YOU'VE ALWAYS BACKED DOWN AND ALWAYS WILL.
SURE, YOU'RE A TERROR WHEN GUTTING UNARMED BRIDES ON THEIR WEDDING NIGHT, OR GUNNING DOWN AN UNCONSCIOUS MAN ON A TOILET.

YOU'RE A COWARD, BLUEBEARD, HIDING BEHIND A LIFETIME OF WEALTH AND PRIVILEGE.
NOW, UNLESS YOU'RE PREPARED TO THROW DOWN...

...I THOUGHT SO, TOUGH GUY.
WHEN YOU GET DONE PISSING YOURSELF WITH FEAR, TUCK TAIL AND DO WHAT I TOLD YOU TO DO.

OBEY ME.

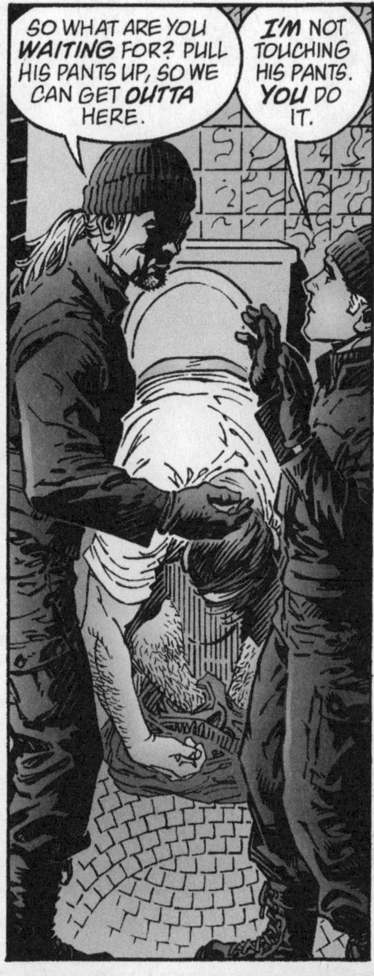
SO WHAT ARE YOU WAITING FOR? PULL HIS PANTS UP, SO WE CAN GET OUTTA HERE.
I'M NOT TOUCHING HIS PANTS. YOU DO IT.

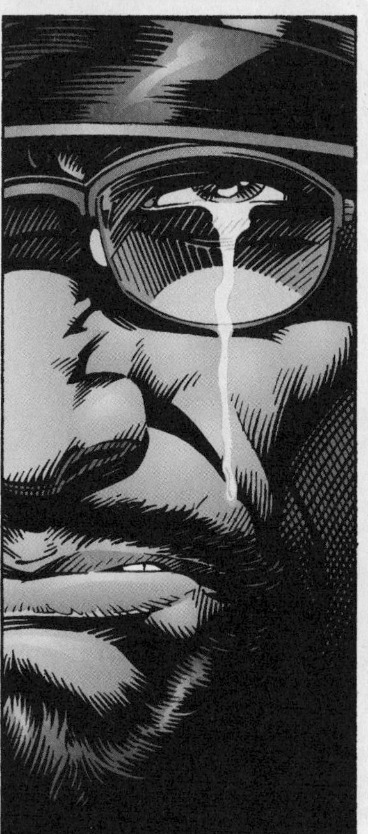

TIME TO WRAP IT UP, KIDS. WE'VE ALREADY BEEN HERE TOO LONG.

MAKE SURE WE'VE GOT EVERYONE AND EVERYTHING WE'RE TAKING WITH US.
Microtek

ALL WE NEED NOW IS FOR SOME MUNDY COP TO COME ALONG AND SEE US HAULING BODIES OUT OF A BUILDING.
HOW LONG ARE THESE THORNS GOING TO CONTINUE TO GROW?
AS LONG AS BRIAR ROSE REMAINS ASLEEP, I THINK. DID SHE GAIN WEIGHT SINCE THE HOMELANDS?

FLYCATCHER, AS **SOON** AS WE GET BACK TO FABLETOWN, ROUND UP A WORKCREW TO COME BACK HERE AND GET **RID** OF THESE THORNS BEFORE THEY GROW MUCH FURTHER.
WHY ME, BIGBY?

BECAUSE YOU'RE THE **ONLY** ONE I TRUST NOT TO FUCK IT UP. BECAUSE WE **CAN'T** ALLOW THE MUNDYS TO WAKE UP AND FIND THEIR BUILDING **COVERED** IN MAGICAL THORNS. OR BECAUSE **I** SAID SO. TAKE YOUR PICK.

GRIMBLE, THIS IS BIGBY WOLF.
RUN UP TO PINOCCHIO'S APARTMENT AND GET HIM FOR ME. IF HE'S ASLEEP, WAKE HIM **UP**. IF HE'S OUT, GO FIND HIM. HE LIKES TO DRINK AT THE BRANSTOCK.
YES, IT'S IMPORTANT. GET **MOVING**.
WILL THE PEOPLE IN THE BUILDING WAKE UP NOW THAT WE'VE TAKEN BRIAR ROSE AWAY?
MAYBE. I DON'T KNOW. IT SHOULDN'T MATTER THOUGH, AS LONG AS THIS TOMMY SHARP CHARACTER **STAYS** ASLEEP.

YOU LOOK **SAD**, MISTER BLUEBEARD. DO YOU FEEL SAD? DID SOMETHING BAD HAPPEN?
SHUT **UP**, YOU RIDICULOUS, INBRED **CRETIN**.

TIME PASSES...
AMNESTY OR NOT, HE HASN'T CHANGED. NO ONE CHANGES HIS BASIC NATURE.

DRESSING HIM UP IN HUMAN SKIN MAKES NO DIFFERENCE. HE'S STILL A PREDA-TORY, MONGREL BEAST.

MAKING HIM OUR SHERIFF ONLY MEANS THAT HE GETS TO HAVE HIS TEETH AROUND EVERYONE'S THROATS AT ONCE.
I WON'T STAND FOR IT ANY LONGER.
OTHER ARM NOW, SIR.

WHAT WILL YOU DO, SIR?
REMOVE HIM, ONCE AND FOR ALL.
YOUR BACK AND BUM NOW, SIR.

CALL IT A COMMUNITY SERVICE.

OKAY, WE'VE DONE WHAT WE NEED TO DO WITH TOMMY SHARP.

LET'S WAKE HER UP.
MY PLEASURE. I WAS WAITING FOR THIS PART.
ALL OF THE MUNDYS ON THE BLOCK COMPLAINED ABOUT THE CHAINSAWS, BUT I JUST KEPT SAYING "MUNICIPAL BUSINESS" OVER AND OVER, LIKE YOU TOLD ME TO.

ANYWAY, WE GOT IT ALL CHOPPED DOWN, BEFORE SUNRISE, BUT THE THORNS KEEP TRYING TO GROW BACK.

SO I LEFT MOST OF THE CREW DOWN THERE TO KEEP ON TOP OF IT, AND CAME BACK TO REPORT IN.

BUT THEY KEEP SENDING GUYS AROUND DE-MANDING TO SEE OUR WORK ORDERS.
NOT NOW, FLYCATCHER. GOOD JOB, BUT NOT NOW.
WHY IS IT TAKING SO LONG? WHY ISN'T SHE WAKING UP?

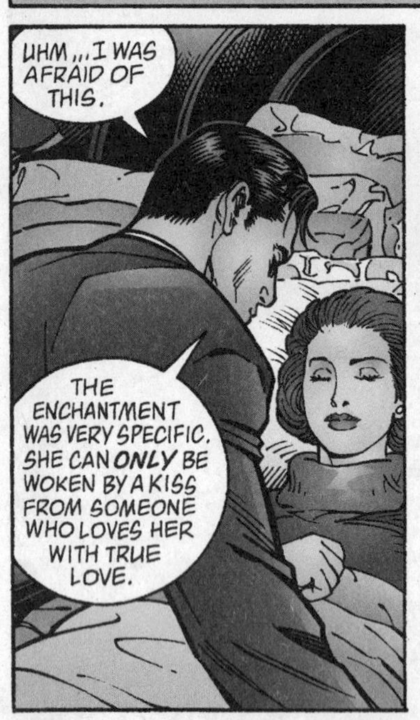
UHM... I WAS AFRAID OF THIS.
THE ENCHANTMENT WAS VERY SPECIFIC. SHE CAN ONLY BE WOKEN BY A KISS FROM SOMEONE WHO LOVES HER WITH TRUE LOVE.

WAY BACK WHEN, THAT DESCRIBED ME. I ALWAYS TRULY LOVE A WOMAN WHEN I'M FIRST CHASING HER. BUT I'M ONLY GOOD AT THE CHASE.
MY LOVE QUICKLY FADED ONCE I HAD TO SETTLE DOWN TO THE TOUGH BUSI-NESS OF ACTUALLY LIVING WITH HER.

I'M JUST NO DAMNED GOOD AT THE HAPPILY EVER AFTER PART.
THEN WHAT DO WE DO? HOW DO WE WAKE HER?

I DON'T KNOW. FIND SOME PRINCE WHO TRULY LOVES HER.
HOW? WE NEED HER AWAKE NOW. WE DON'T HAVE TIME TO GO LOOKING FOR...

EXCUSE ME, MISTER WOLF. *I* COULD TRY.
NOT NOW, FLY. THIS IS GROWN-UP TALK. WE NEED TO BE **SERIOUS** NOW.

BUT I **AM** SERIOUS. YOU NEED A PRINCE AND I'M A PRINCE. MAYBE NOT A VERY HANDSOME ONE, BUT I'M AWFULLY FOND OF MISS BRIAR. I MEAN SHE'S... I TAKE ONE LOOK AT HER AND I WANT TO,,,
...WHO WOULDN'T?

WHAT THE HELL. WHY NOT? GIVE IT A SHOT.
ARE YOU OUT OF YOUR ***MIND?*** HE'S AN IMBECILE!

LET HIM TRY. WHAT COULD IT ***HURT?***

I'LL BE ***DAMNED***. IT WORKED.
WHAT ***HAPPENED?*** UHM,,,HOW DID IT ALL TURN OUT? AND WHY DOES MY MOUTH TASTE LIKE ***BUGS?***
CAN'T TALK NOW. SHARP WILL BE WAKING.

TIME TO WAKE UP, TOMMY BOY.

OH GOD. MY HEAD.
WHAT HAPPENED TO ME?
I FEEL LIKE SOMEONE SLIPPED ME A MICKEY.
WHICH IS MORE OR LESS WHAT WE DID.

OH MY GOD! IT'S YOU!
HOW DID YOU GET ME? WHAT DID YOU DO?
HERE. LOOK AT YOURSELF IN THIS. LOOK AT YOUR NECK.

WHAT DID YOU SICK CREATURES DO TO ME?

YOU FIGURED OUT WE'RE VAMPIRES, TOMMY. YOU KNOW WHAT WE DID. WE DRANK YOUR BLOOD.
OH DEAR LORDY.

NOT ALL THAT MUCH. NOT ENOUGH TO CHANGE YOU INTO ONE OF US. **RELAX.** YOU WON'T BE GROWING FANGS OR AVOIDING ITALIAN FOOD.

BUT NOW WE'LL BE ABLE TO KEEP TABS ON YOU, AND CONTROL YOU IF WE HAVE TO. YOU'VE SEEN THE MOVIES, YOU **KNOW** HOW THAT WORKS.
I ONLY WANTED A BIG STORY. I DIDN'T **MEAN** ANYTHING.

YOU TRIED TO SELL US OUT FOR A FEW DAYS OF FLEETING NOTORIETY. WE DON'T **ALLOW** THAT SORT OF THING.
WHAT ARE YOU PLANNING TO DO WITH ME?

NOTHING, AS LONG AS YOU BEHAVE. BUT IF YOU EXPOSE US, WE'LL MAKE YOU DO SOMETHING **FATAL** TO YOURSELF. HANG YOURSELF. SLIT YOUR WRISTS IN THE BATH.
WHATEVER STRIKES OUR **FANCY** AT THE TIME. WE'VE TASTED YOUR **BLOOD**. YOU WON'T BE ABLE TO RESIST US.

I WASN'T TRYING TO **HURT** YOU PEOPLE. I **LIKED** YOU. I DID. I'VE BEEN GETTING CLOSER AND CLOSER TO YOU FOR THREE YEARS. LEARNING YOUR STORIES AND RELATIONSHIPS.
BUT IT WAS SUCH A BIG STORY.

IT'S NO STORY AT ALL NOW. AND SHARPIE, IF YOU'VE ALREADY SENT IT TO SOMEONE...
...IF **ANY** PART OF YOUR STORY GETS OUT, EVEN FROM SOMEONE ELSE, WE'LL DO **MORE** THAN KILL YOU.

WE'LL DESTROY YOUR REPUTATION. WE'LL MAKE YOUR KIDS, YOUR FAMILY AND BOTH OF YOUR EX-WIVES **DETEST** YOU.
AND ALL YOUR LOYAL READERS, TOO.
WH-WHY? HOW? WHAT ARE YOU GOING TO DO?

LOOK AT THESE. KEEP THEM IF YOU LIKE. WE'VE GOT **COPIES**.
AGPA

OH NO.

WHAT HAVE YOU DONE?
WHAT DID YOU MAKE ME DO?

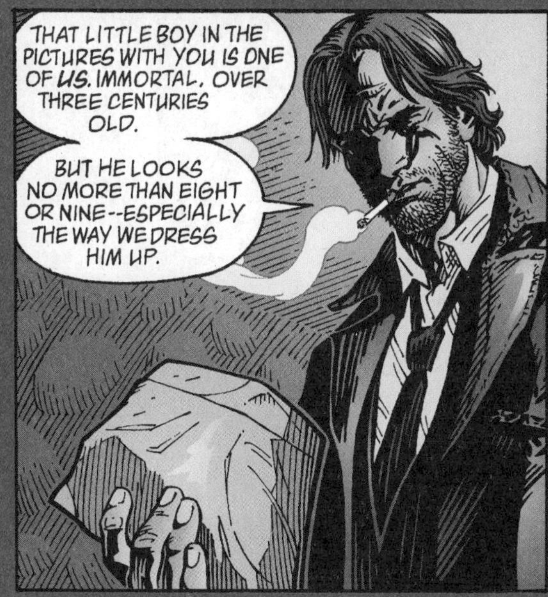
THAT LITTLE BOY IN THE PICTURES WITH YOU IS ONE OF US. IMMORTAL, OVER THREE CENTURIES OLD.
BUT HE LOOKS NO MORE THAN EIGHT OR NINE--ESPECIALLY THE WAY WE DRESS HIM UP.

I NEVER DID THIS. I'M NOT--
I COULDN'T HAVE.
WHAT WILL PEOPLE THINK OF YOU WHEN THESE GET OUT? EVEN IN OUR LIBERTINE ERA THIS SORT OF CONDUCT IS NOTHING SHORT OF DISGUSTING.

HERE'S HIS EXTENSIVE AND DETAILED FORENSIC INTERVIEW WITH A CHILD PSYCHOLOGIST.
TWO SOLID HOURS-WORTH. YOU'LL ESPECIALLY LOVE THE PART WHERE HE POINTS OUT ON HIS FAVORITE TEDDY BEAR ALL THE IN-APPROPRIATE PLACES YOU TOUCHED HIM.

HE'S VERY CONVINCING.

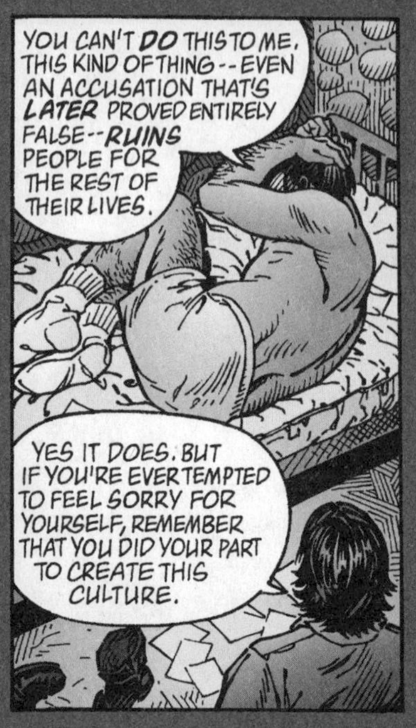
YOU CAN'T DO THIS TO ME. THIS KIND OF THING -- EVEN AN ACCUSATION THAT'S LATER PROVED ENTIRELY FALSE -- RUINS PEOPLE FOR THE REST OF THEIR LIVES.
YES IT DOES. BUT IF YOU'RE EVER TEMPTED TO FEEL SORRY FOR YOURSELF, REMEMBER THAT YOU DID YOUR PART TO CREATE THIS CULTURE.

WELCOME TO THE WORLD YOU MADE, YOU PATHETIC LITTLE MEDIA FUCK.

WHAT DO I HAVE TO DO?
NOTHING.
GO BACK TO YOUR LIFE AND FORGET ALL ABOUT US, FOREVER. MAKE SURE NO ONE EVER FINDS OUT ABOUT US, EVEN AFTER YOUR NATURAL DEATH -- IF YOU CARE ABOUT HOW YOU'RE REMEMBERED.

COME IN HERE, JACK.
AFTER THIS PIECE OF SHIT GETS DRESSED, ESCORT HIM OUT AND PUT HIM IN A CAB. MAKE SURE HE TAKES THE VIDEOTAPE AND ALL OF HIS DIRTY PICTURES WITH HIM.
SURE THING, SHERIFF.

YOU'LL WANT TO TAKE A GOOD LOOK AT THOSE, TOMMY, EVERY TIME YOU'RE TEMPTED TO PLAY JOURNALIST AGAIN.

IF YOU PUBLISH, WE PUBLISH. SIMPLE AS THAT.

AND AT THAT MOMENT...
GOLD-PLATED MOOREWOOD AND BERMAN BATHROOM FIXTURES.

VENETIAN MARBLE TILES AND COUNTER-TOPS.

ETRUSCAN STATUARY.

SUNG DYNASTY CERAMICS. OH, BRIAR, MY LOST LOVE --
--YOU **HAVE** DONE WELL FOR YOURSELF.

I DON'T THINK YOU SHOULD BE GETTING UP **YET**, BRIAR, DEAR.

YOU NEED TO LIE DOWN UNTIL YOU FEEL BETTER AGAIN.
I'M OKAY. JUST A LITTLE DISORIENTED IS ALL.

MY SLEEPING SPELLS SOMETIMES LEAVE ME FEELING THIS WAY.

THAT'S FINE. YOU'RE SAFE AND AT HOME AND IN GOOD HANDS.
WE'LL JUST SIT HERE UNTIL IT PASSES.
WHY ARE YOU STILL HERE?

SOMEONE HAD TO STAY TO LOOK AFTER YOU.

WHY ARE YOU **SMILING** LIKE THAT?

"NO REASON. JUST AN AMUSING LITTLE SOMETHING SOMEONE TOLD ME RECENTLY."
I GOT ALL THE SECURITY TAPES. NOW WE JUST HAVE TO WAIT FOR THEM TO FINISH UPSTAIRS.
LOOK AT HER, FLY.
SHE ALWAYS DID LOOK HER BEST WHEN SHE WAS SLEEP-ING.
SHE IS REAL PRETTY, MISTER CHARMING. AND RICH TOO.
THAT ALWAYS HELPS.
SERIOUSLY? BRIAR ROSE GOT OUT WITH HER FORTUNE INTACT? I NEVER HEARD THAT.
NAW, SHE SHOWED UP HERE AS POOR AS THE REST OF US. BUT THAT DIDN'T LAST LONG.
REMEMBER ALL THOSE FAIRY BLESSINGS SHE GOT ON HER CHRISTENING DAY? ONE OF THEM WAS THAT SHE'D ALWAYS BE WEALTHY. WITHIN A YEAR OF ARRIVING HERE SHE MADE A KILLING IN THE STOCK MARKET. BIG MAGIC, Y'KNOW?
DO TELL.
IF SHE GAVE IT ALL AWAY TODAY, SHE'D PROBABLY WIN THE LOTTERY TOMORROW.
WHO'S SHE SEEING THESE DAYS?

WHY ARE YOU SUDDENLY BEING SO NICE TO ME? WHAT ARE YOU UP TO?
IT'S NOT ALL THAT SUDDEN, DEAR. WE JUST HAVEN'T SOCIALIZED SINCE ESCAPING THE HOMELANDS. I KNOW WE ENDED OUR MARRIAGE BADLY, AND IT WAS ENTIRELY MY FAULT. I WAS UNFIT FOR THE HOLY STATE OF MATRIMONY.
BUT SINCE THEN I'VE BEEN INFECTED BY THE SPIRIT OF THE GENERAL AMNESTY. WE'VE EACH TAKEN A PUBLIC STAND ON THE SIDE OF FORGIVENESS AND A NEW CLEAN SLATE.

I HAVE TO CONFESS, I FIND MYSELF IN AWE OF YOUR GENEROSITY OF HEART.
BUT THAT DOESN'T APPLY TO...
AND YOU ARE TO BE ADMIRED MOST OF ALL, BECAUSE YOU AND I BOTH KNOW YOU'VE HAD THE MOST TO FORGIVE.

BUT...
MY THOUGHTS EXACTLY. BUT I CAN'T JUST BLITHELY ACCEPT YOUR FORGIVENESS AND MOVE ON WITHOUT ANY ACT OF CONTRITION ON MY PART.
THE OLD PRINCE CHARMING MIGHT HAVE BEEN ABLE TO, BUT THAT MAN NO LONGER EXISTS.

I'M RESOLVED TO EARN WHAT YOU'VE SO FREELY GIVEN ME.
AND AS MY PENANCE, I'M GOING TO STAY HERE WITH YOU--NO, NOT ROMANTICALLY--THOSE DAYS ARE PAST US NOW. I NO LONGER DESERVE THOSE GLORIES.

SO I'LL STAY HERE PLATONICALLY, IN ONE OF THE OTHER BED-ROOMS, AND TAKE CARE OF YOU.
SEE YOU THROUGH YOUR SPELLS, FOR MONTHS, YEARS, OR DECADES--AS LONG AS IT TAKES TO WORK OFF MY DEBT.
BUT...

DAYS PASS...
YOU LET HIM MOVE IN WITH YOU?

IT'S NOT LIKE THAT. HE'S IN A GUEST ROOM.
THE BIGGEST ONE, I'LL BET.
CAN WE PLEASE GET TO WHY YOU ASKED ME HERE, MISTER WOLF?
I'M JUST CATCHING UP ON SOME PAPERWORK AND ONE DETAIL NAGGED AT ME ABOUT YOUR INCIDENT BACK IN TIFFANY'S. WE HAD SOME TROUBLE WAKING YOU LAST WEEK AFTER THE SHARP AFFAIR.

BUT I NEVER FOUND OUT HOW THEY WOKE YOU THEN-- IN THAT PUBLIC STORE --AND HOW NO ONE NOTICED ANYTHING ODD ABOUT IT.

ONE OF THE ...UH... POLICEMEN WHO RESPONDED TO THE SITUATION --HE HAD A POLICE DOG.
A VERY AFFECTIONATE POLICE DOG. I WOKE TO HIM LAPPING AT MY FACE.
AND DON'T TELL ME -- THE DOG'S NAME WAS PRINCE?

REPEAT ANY OF THIS AND I'LL HATE YOU FOREVER.

I DON'T HAVE MUCH CHOICE, **DO** I? YOU GUYS SAY "JUMP" AND I ASK "HOW HIGH?"

EXACTLY RIGHT.

I THOUGHT WE SHOULD HAVE AN UPDATE ON THE STATE OF YOUR NOTES, FILES AND OTHER EVIDENCE PERTAINING TO MY COMMUNITY.

IT'S DESTROYED. **ALL** OF IT. NO NOTES. NO TRACES. NOTHING. YOU CAN SEARCH ME, OR MY PLACE--ANYWHERE YOU LIKE.

OH, THAT WON'T BE NECESSARY, THOMAS.

POW!

I BELIEVE YOU.

AND WE'LL ALL SLEEP MORE COMFORTABLY AT NIGHT WITHOUT THAT UGLY BUSINESS HANGING OVER OUR HEADS ANY LONGER.

FABLES

STORYBOOK LOVE 1

Cover art by James Jean

IT LOOKS LIKE THE COAST IS CLEAR, SARGE.
THEN MOVE OUT, CORPORAL.
AND LET'S GET THIS DISTASTEFUL BUSINESS OVER WITH, BEFORE SOMEONE RETURNS TO CATCH US.

The Mouse Police Never Sleep
Storybook Love
Part One
Bill Willingham
writer/creator
Mark Buckingham
penciller
Steve Leialoha
inker
Daniel Vozzo
color/separations
Todd Klein
letterer
James Jean
cover art
Mariah Huehner
assistant editor
Shelly Bond
editor
SPRINGTIME IN FABLETOWN, AND ALL IS RIGHT WITH THE WORLD.
NOD'S BOOKS
LEWIS ANTIQUES
GOOD AFTERNOON, SHERIFF. GOOD AFTERNOON, MISS WHITE. IT'S GREAT TO SEE YOU OUT AND ABOUT AGAIN.
VISIT OUR COMICS NOOK
NEW IN THIS WEEK
TIRED OF MY COMPANY SO SOON?
COMPANY IS ONE THING, MISTER WOLF. MONTHS OF CONSTANT HOVERING IS SOMETHING ELSE ENTIRELY.
I WANT THINGS BACK TO NORMAL. YOU BACK IN YOUR OFFICE AND ME IN MINE.
EASY ENOUGH FOR YOU, WITH AN OFFICE THE SIZE OF A--WHO KNOWS HOW BIG IT ACTUALLY IS? MOST OF THE BRANCHING PASSAGES STILL HAVEN'T BEEN EXPLORED.
TODAYS SPECIAL

ARE YOU SURE YOU'RE READY TO DO THIS, SNOW?
YOU SAID YOU'D STOP BABYING ME THE DAY I COULD WALK THREE TIMES UP AND DOWN BULLFINCH STREET, UNDER MY OWN POWER, WITHOUT NEEDING THE WHEEL-CHAIR.
WELL, COME HELL OR HIGH WATER, THIS IS THAT DAY, AFTER WHICH I'M DAMN WELL GOING TO HOLD YOU TO YOUR PROMISE.
I AM THE EGGMAN
TODAY'S SPECIAL CURDS & WHEY
WE'LL GET TO IT SOMEDAY.
MEANWHILE I'M STUCK IN THAT BOX THAT MAKES A CLOSET LOOK SPACIOUS.
NOD'S BOOKS
OPEN
POOR BIGBY. YOU CAN STILL VISIT ME ONCE A WEEK FOR OUR REGULAR SECURITY BRIEFING.
SPEAKING OF WHICH, WHY DON'T YOU FILL ME IN NOW, AS LONG AS I'M STUCK DOING MY LAPS?
NOT MUCH TO REPORT. NONE OF THE FABLES LIVING ABROAD IN THE WIDE WORLD SEEM TO BE ACTING UP.
THIS ACCORDING TO YOUR SO-CALLED "TOURISTS"?
EDWARD BEAR'S CANDIES
FORD

GATHER AROUND, STUDENTS.
CHATEAU D'IF FENCING ACADEMY
GRAND GREEN FLORIST SHOP
YES, MA'AM, BUT I REMIND YOU THAT WITH ONLY THREE FIELD AGENTS TO COVER THE ENTIRE MUNDY WORLD, I CAN HARDLY GUARANTEE--
FORGET IT, BIGBY. WE ARE NOT TURNING THIS INTO ANOTHER GRIPE SESSION ABOUT YOUR OPERATING BUDGET.

I HAVE A SPECIAL TREAT FOR YOU TODAY.
A DEMONSTRATION OF ADVANCED SWORDSMANSHIP FROM TWO ACKNOWLEDGED EXPERTS IN THE ART.

ONE OF THEM YOU ALREADY KNOW WELL. LORD BLUEBEARD HAS GENEROUSLY DONATED HIS TIME AS ONE OF OUR GUEST INSTRUCTORS, OVER THE MANY YEARS.

WE COULD SWITCH OUT THESE TOYS FOR REAL BLADES, IF YOU'D PREFER, YOUR HIGHNESS--AND FENCE TO FIRST BLOOD?
BUT YOU'VE NEVER BEFORE SEEN A TRUE DEMONSTRATION OF HIS SKILLS--
--BECAUSE WE'VE NEVER BEFORE HAD ACCESS TO A CHALLENGER WORTHY OF HIS BEST EFFORTS... UNTIL NOW.
GIVE THESE KIDS A REAL SHOW?
THIS AFTERNOON WE'RE FORTUNATE TO BE VISITED BY ANOTHER FAMOUS MASTER OF BLADES, PRINCE CHARMING...
...WHO'S ONLY RECENTLY TAKEN UP FULL-TIME RESIDENCE IN FABLETOWN.
SO PAY ATTENTION. AND LEARN SOMETHING.
OH NO, DREAD LORD. THAT'S FAR TOO MUCH DRAMA FOR AN AFTERNOON'S LIGHT ROMP.
FOILS WILL DO FOR NOW.
ARE YOU READY, GENTLEMEN?
YES.
ALWAYS.
THEN BEGIN.

I TAKE IT YOU DON'T LIKE ESPIONAGE MISSIONS, SERGEANT WILFRED?
BRANSTOCK TAVERN
THE GLASS SLIPPER SHOES
YELLOW
WEB N'

NO, I MOST CERTAINLY *DON'T*. GENTLEMEN SHOULD NOT READ EACH OTHER'S MAIL.

BUT SINCE WE CAN'T PICK AND *CHOOSE* WHICH DUTIES WE'RE CALLED TO PERFORM...
IT GETS US AWAY FROM THE FARM AT LEAST.

I'D MUCH RATHER STAY UP ON THE FARM, PATROLLING SMALLTOWN'S BORDERS. EVERY TIME WE'RE SENT DOWN TO THE CITY, WE END UP WORKING FOR ONE GULLIVER SPYING ON ANOTHER.

HALT!
TOUCH! ON-TARGET!
FIRST SCORE TO LORD BLUEBEARD!

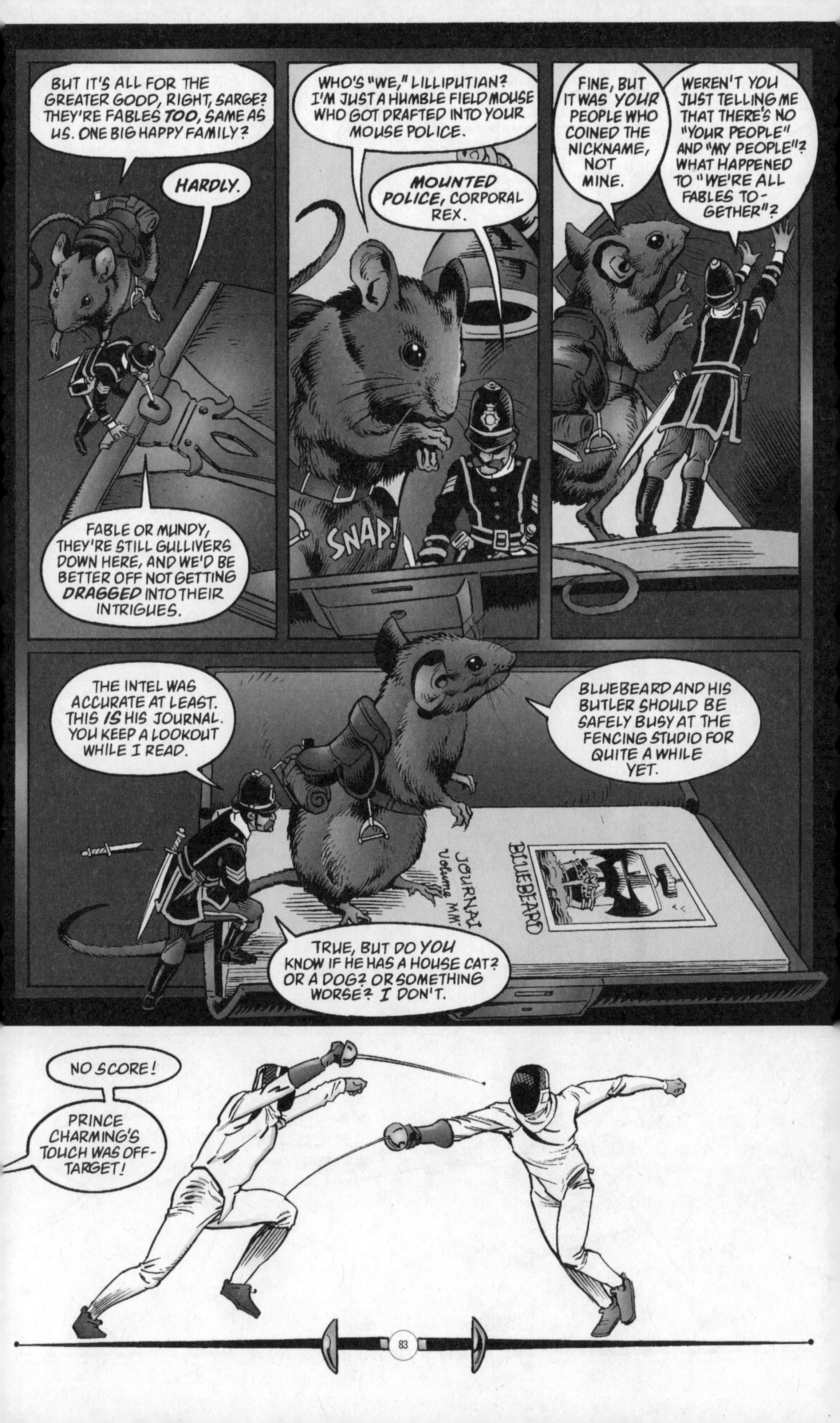
BUT IT'S ALL FOR THE GREATER GOOD, RIGHT, SARGE? THEY'RE FABLES TOO, SAME AS US. ONE BIG HAPPY FAMILY?
HARDLY.
FABLE OR MUNDY, THEY'RE STILL GULLIVERS DOWN HERE, AND WE'D BE BETTER OFF NOT GETTING DRAGGED INTO THEIR INTRIGUES.
WHO'S "WE," LILLIPUTIAN? I'M JUST A HUMBLE FIELD MOUSE WHO GOT DRAFTED INTO YOUR MOUSE POLICE.
MOUNTED POLICE, CORPORAL REX.
SNAP!
FINE, BUT IT WAS YOUR PEOPLE WHO COINED THE NICKNAME, NOT MINE.
WEREN'T YOU JUST TELLING ME THAT THERE'S NO "YOUR PEOPLE" AND "MY PEOPLE"? WHAT HAPPENED TO "WE'RE ALL FABLES TO-GETHER"?
THE INTEL WAS ACCURATE AT LEAST. THIS IS HIS JOURNAL. YOU KEEP A LOOKOUT WHILE I READ.
BLUEBEARD AND HIS BUTLER SHOULD BE SAFELY BUSY AT THE FENCING STUDIO FOR QUITE A WHILE YET.
JOURNAL Volume MM
BLUEBEARD
TRUE, BUT DO YOU KNOW IF HE HAS A HOUSE CAT? OR A DOG? OR SOMETHING WORSE? I DON'T.
NO SCORE!
PRINCE CHARMING'S TOUCH WAS OFF-TARGET!

THINGS ARE MORE OR LESS BACK TO NORMAL AT THE FARM.
"YOUR SISTER SEEMS TO BE DOING A HALF-DECENT JOB OF RUNNING IT."
NO, JACK, YOU MAY NOT COME UP HERE TO SEE ME.
BECAUSE YOU AND I AREN'T TOGETHER ANYMORE.
WE'VE GOT MORE SILAGE CORN THAN WE NEED FOR THE COMING YEAR, ROSE, BUT WE'RE GOING TO COME UP SHORT ON WINTER WHEAT AND SWEET CORN.
BECAUSE YOU WEREN'T A VERY GOOD BOYFRIEND--
--EXCEPT TO THE EXTENT THAT YOU WERE USEFUL IN HELPING ME ANNOY THE HELL OUT OF MY SISTER.
DAIRY AND EGG PRODUCTION IS UP--EXCEPT FOR GOAT'S MILK.
ON TARGET!
BLUEBEARD LEADS, TWO TO ZERO!

BUT MY LIFE ISN'T ABOUT WHAT WILL BOTHER SNOW WHITE ANYMORE. IT'S ABOUT WHAT'S BEST FOR ME. AND FACE IT, JACKALOPE, WE APPEALED TO THE VERY WORST IN EACH OTHER.
"ROSE HAS BLOSSOMED, NOW THAT SHE'S FINALLY OUT FROM UNDER YOUR SHADOW."
THE GOATS HAVE BEEN FIGHTING WITH THE TROLLS AGAIN.
CAN YOU KEEP THE EDITORIALIZING TO A MINIMUM, PLEASE?
DO YOU KNOW TIJUANA TAXI?
YEP, BUT YOU'LL NEVER HEAR ME PLAY IT IN THIS LIFETIME.
YELLOW BRICK ROAD HOUSE
YELLOW BRICK ROAD HOUSE FULL DINNER AND LUNCH MENU
ANYTHING YOU SAY, BOSS. GOLDILOCKS REMAINS AT LARGE, AND THE TRAIL HAS GONE WELL AND TRULY COLD.
THINGS ARE ALSO SECURE HERE ON THE HOME FRONT, EXCEPT--
YES? WHAT IS IT?
--I'M NOT SURE IF THIS FALLS UNDER THE UMBRELLA OF "OFFICIAL BUSINESS," OR IF IT ONLY QUALIFIES AS GOSSIP, BUT--
WILL YOU JUST GET TO IT?
TOUCH!
THREE TO NOTHING, BLUEBEARD'S FAVOR.
FOUR TO ZERO!

"PRINCE CHARMING HAS MOVED IN WITH WIFE NUMBER THREE, BRIAR ROSE. BUT ONLY IN ONE OF HER GUEST ROOMS SO FAR, ACCORDING TO MY SOURCES."
I ADDED SOME THINGS TO YOUR SHOPPING LIST, BRIAR, SO I'LL NEED MORE MONEY THIS TIME.
NO, OUR SLEEPING BEAUTY WAS WIFE NUMBER TWO. FIRST ME, THEN BRIAR, THEN CINDERELLA.
OKAY. IN ANY CASE HE SEEMS TO HAVE TAKEN UP WITH HER AGAIN.
TAKEN UP WITH HER FAT BANK ACCOUNT IS MORE LIKE IT.
NONE OF MY CONCERN THOUGH-- AS LONG AS IT KEEPS HIM OUT OF MY HAIR. IF SHE CAN PUT UP WITH HIM, MORE POWER TO BOTH OF THEM.
THAT'S A GOOD ATTITUDE, SNOW-- KEEPING YOURSELF CLEAR OF ANY FURTHER ENTANGLEMENTS WITH THAT LOTHARIO.
WHICH OF COURSE KEEPS YOU FREE TO RECEIVE GENTLEMEN CALLERS OF BETTER CHARACTER-- ALTHOUGH WITH LESS REFINEMENT THAN YOU'RE USED TO.
MY GOD, WILL YOU LET IT DROP ONCE AND FOR ALL? HOW MANY WAYS CAN I POSSIBLY EXPLAIN TO YOU THAT I'M NOT INTERESTED? THE CUPBOARD IS BARE. NO BONE FOR THE OLD DOG.
I DON'T KNOW, PRINCESS, BUT KEEP TRYING UNTIL YOU COME UP WITH ONE THAT ACTUALLY CONVINCES YOU--OOPS, I MEAN ME.

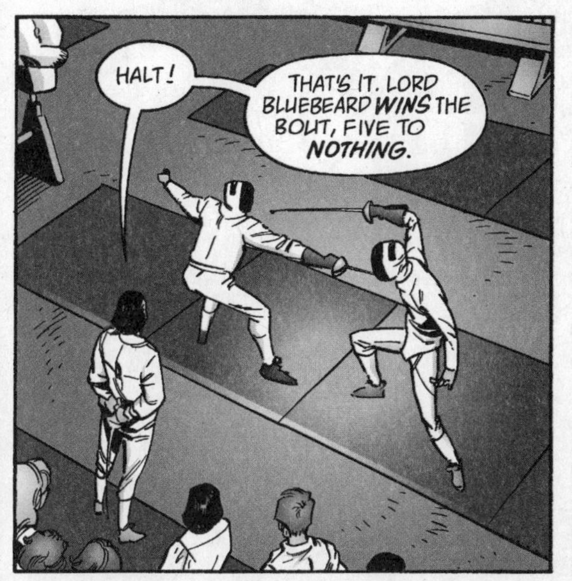
HALT!
THAT'S IT. LORD BLUEBEARD WINS THE BOUT, FIVE TO NOTHING.

HA! A CLEAN SWEEP!
CONGRATULATIONS, BLUEBEARD.

YOU DID FINE, OF COURSE. YOU WERE JUST OUT OF PRACTICE. HARD TO TRAIN, WHAT WITH YOUR RECENT TRAVELS.
WELL DONE. NOTHING TO BE ASHAMED OF.
SURE. FINE.

NOW, IF YOU'LL EXCUSE ME--

I SUPPOSE HIS HIGHNESS WILL GET OVER IT, GIVEN TIME.
COME ALONG, HOBBES. IT'S GETTING LATE AND I WANT YOU TO DRAW ME A BATH BEFORE SUPPER.
VERY GOOD, SIR.

YOU SHOULD TELL YOUR MANSERVANT HOBBES THAT HE DOESN'T NEED TO PUT HIS GLAMOUR UP EVERY TIME I SEE HIM.
I'M NO HOMOCENTRIC SPECIES BIGOT.
AND I'M HARDLY A SHRINKING VIOLET, TO WILT AT THE SIGHT OF A GOBLIN MALE IN HIS NATURAL STATE.
HOBBES' NATURAL STATE WAS SACKED BY THE ADVERSARY, JUST AS YOURS AND MINE WERE, GOLDI-LOCKS.
YOU KNOW WHAT I MEANT.
YES, AND I KNOW THE INCREASINGLY OVERT SUGGESTIONS YOU'VE BEEN MAKING TO HOBBES EVERY TIME HE'S HAD TO VISIT YOUR ROOMS.
HE TOLD YOU?

HE TELLS ME EVERYTHING, AND HE'S NOT COMFORTABLE WITH YOUR BEHAVIOR OF LATE.
NOT INTERESTED IN WOMEN, HUH?
AT LEAST NOT HUMAN WOMEN, SO PLEASE LEAVE HIM ALONE. HE HAS HIS DUTIES TO ATTEND TO.
BUT I'M BORED, LOCKED AWAY HERE IN THIS DREARY PLACE. YOU TWO ARE THE ONLY OTHER PEOPLE I'VE SEEN IN MONTHS.
I NEED MY DISTRACTIONS. AND I'M USED TO MORE VARIETY IN MY-- I MEAN YOU'RE FINE AND ALL, BUT--
IT CAN'T BE HELPED. YOU'RE NOT SAFE ANYWHERE ELSE. BY NOW EVERY FABLE IN THIS STATE IS ON THE LOOKOUT FOR YOU.
OH MY.
GOLDILOCKS! HERE?!

SO, WHEN ARE YOU GOING TO LET ME IN ON YOUR PLAN TO GET ME TO SAFETY--AND MORE IMPORTANT--WHAT'S IT GOING TO COST ME? MORE THAN THE OCCASIONAL BLOW JOB, I SUSPECT.
LET'S MOVE OUT, CORPORAL REX. THIS NEEDS REPORTING IMMEDIATELY.
LOTS MORE.
ENOUGH TO OFFSET THE TERRIBLE RISK I'M TAKING BY HIDING YOU.
HUH?!
I SAID, IT WOULD COST YOU ENOUGH TO OFFSET--
NOT YOU! I SAW SOMETHING! A MOUSE!
DON'T WORRY, LOVE. I'LL PROTECT YOU FROM THE BIG, BAD MOUSE.

IT WASN'T JUST A MOUSE, YOU FOOL! I THINK IT HAD A RIDER! IT'S THE GODDAMN MOUNTED POLICE!
HELP ME CATCH IT, OR KILL IT, OR WE'LL BOTH HANG!
BUT--!
THERE THEY GO!
RUN LIKE THE WIND, REX!
SCREW THE WIND!

I COULD OUTRUN THE WIND ON MY WORST DAY.
THIS WAY!
OOF!
GET UP, YOU OAF! THEY'RE GETTING AWAY!
SO YOU SAY. I'VE YET TO SEE ANY-THING.

THERE'S OUR EXIT.
I SEE IT.

WE MADE IT, SARGE! HURRAH FOR US!

THWUNK
REX!

GET OUT OF HERE, BOSS. I'M DONE FOR.
BUT--
DO YOUR DUTY, DAMN IT.

AND WHAT HAVE WE HERE?

CURIOUS INDEED.

SEE THE SADDLE? THEY WERE MOUNTED POLICE SPIES, ALL RIGHT.
BUT WHO WOULD THEY HAVE BEEN SPYING FOR?
SNOW WHITE OR BIGBY. EITHER WAY, WE'RE DEAD AS SOON AS THIS THING'S PARTNER REACHES ONE OF THEM TO REPORT WHAT HE SAW.
SO WHAT WILL YOU DO, SIR?

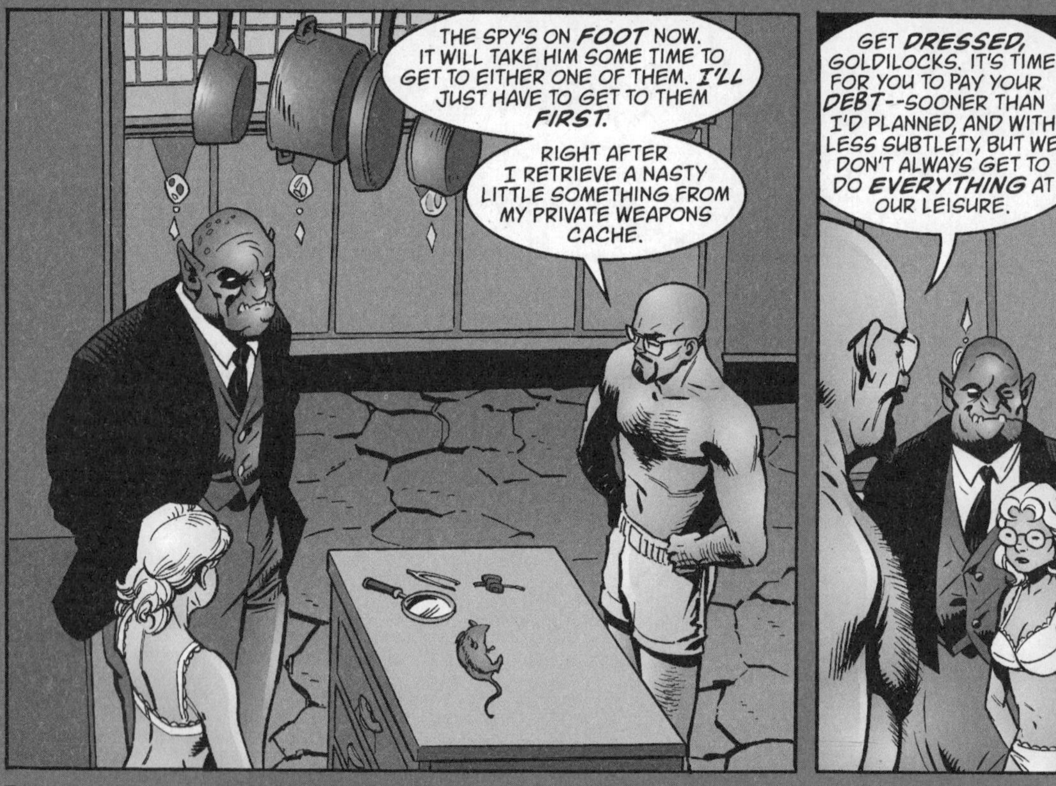
THE SPY'S ON FOOT NOW. IT WILL TAKE HIM SOME TIME TO GET TO EITHER ONE OF THEM. I'LL JUST HAVE TO GET TO THEM FIRST.
RIGHT AFTER I RETRIEVE A NASTY LITTLE SOMETHING FROM MY PRIVATE WEAPONS CACHE.
GET DRESSED, GOLDILOCKS. IT'S TIME FOR YOU TO PAY YOUR DEBT--SOONER THAN I'D PLANNED, AND WITH LESS SUBTLETY, BUT WE DON'T ALWAYS GET TO DO EVERYTHING AT OUR LEISURE.

OKAY, WE'RE HERE.

NOW WILL YOU TELL US WHAT'S SO IMPORTANT YOU HAD TO DRAG US BOTH OUT OF BED LONG BEFORE NORMAL BUSINESS HOURS?

YOU'LL BE GLAD I DID, MISS WHITE. LOOK AT THIS.
OKAY, I'LL BITE. WHAT IS IT?

SOMETHING JACK TRIED TO SELL ME LAST NIGHT AT THE BRANSTOCK.
HE CLAIMS IT'S HIGHLY MAGICAL AND HE CAN SUPPLY A CASE OF THEM.

IN CLEAR VIOLATION OF THE RE-QUIREMENT TO TURN IN ALL SIG-NIFICANT MAGIC ARTIFACTS FOR COMMUNAL OWNERSHIP AND SAFE STORAGE IN THE BUSINESS OFFICE.
AND WAIT UNTIL YOU SEE WHAT IT DOES.
HEY, MAYBE YOU SHOULDN'T--

--DO THAT.
SON OF A--
ALL BETTER NOW? LISTEN UP THEN. HERE ARE YOUR ORDERS FOR THE NEXT FEW DAYS...
A BIT LATER...
AND REMEMBER, IF BY CHANCE YOU MANAGE TO SURVIVE, EVERYTHING WAS JACK'S FAULT.
SECURITY OFFICE
B. WOLF

AND LATER STILL...
MISS WHITE, WHAT AN UNEXPECTED PLEASURE TO SEE YOU. COME IN.
I DON'T RECALL THAT WE HAD A MEETING SCHEDULED. IS EVERYTHING ALL RIGHT? SOME NEW CRISIS LOOMING?
NO, EVERYTHING'S FINE, SIR. SO MUCH SO, IN FACT, THAT I'VE DECIDED TO GO ON VACATION.

I MUST HAVE SEVERAL HUNDRED VACATION DAYS SAVED UP BY NOW.
WELL, YES, BUT-- YOU **NEVER** TAKE VACATIONS. THIS IS-- UHM, WHERE DO YOU PLAN TO GO?

I'M NOT SURE. MAYBE I'LL TRY THE TABLES IN LAS VEGAS, OR LIE ON THE BEACH IN CANCUN.
NO-- BETTER YET, SOMEWHERE NO PHONES CAN REACH ME. MAYBE I'LL GO CAMPING SOMEWHERE FAR AND REMOTE.

I TOLD BOY BLUE TO CONSULT YOU IF ANYTHING IMPORTANT COMES UP WHILE I'M GONE.
CONSULT ME? WHY ME? THAT'S **NOT** OUR SYSTEM. WHY NOT BIGBY WOLF?

OH, DIDN'T I TELL YOU? HE'S COMING **TOO.** HE ALSO HAS VACATION DAYS.

IT TURNS OUT WE DESPERATELY WANT TO GO AWAY TOGETHER.

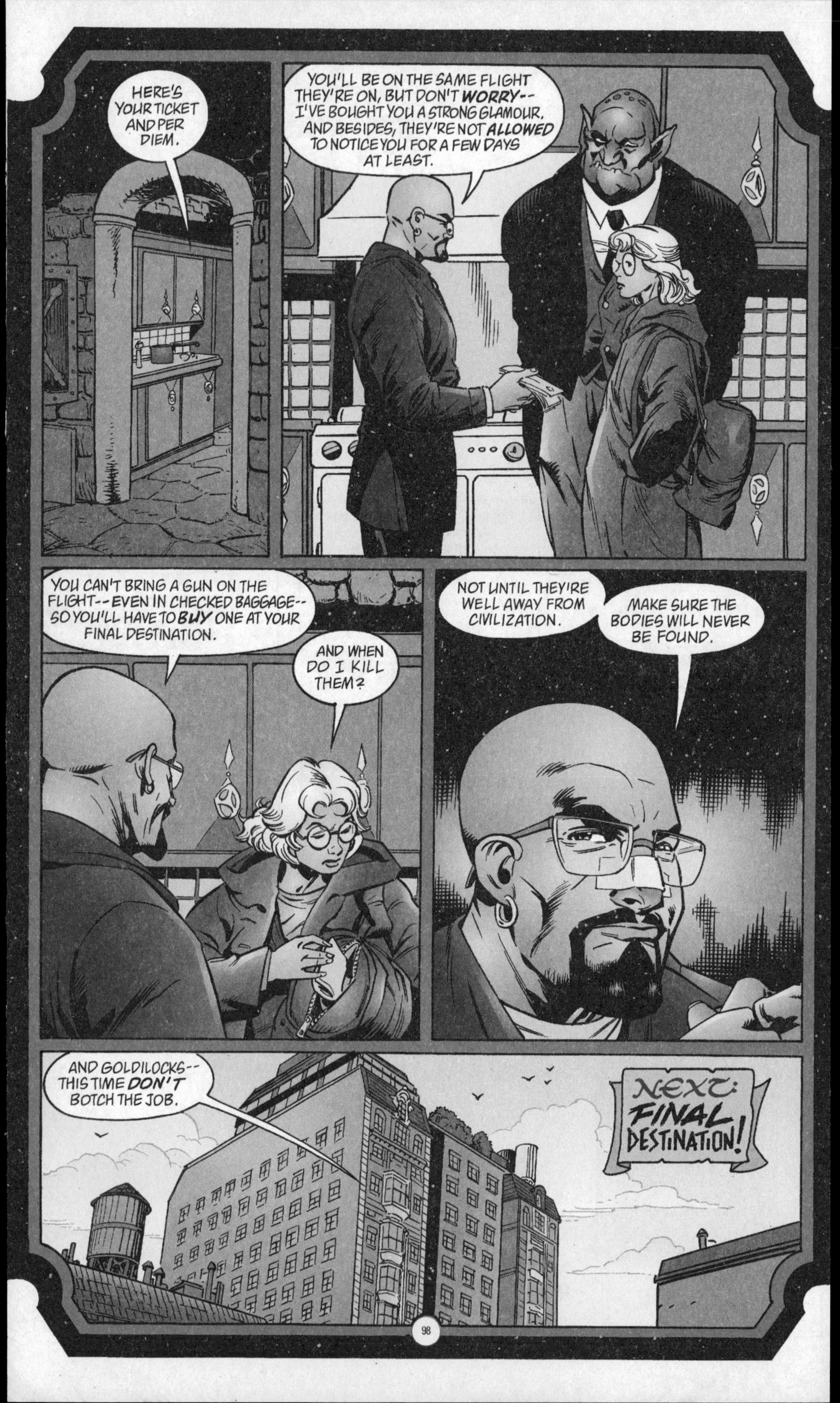
HERE'S YOUR TICKET AND PER DIEM.
YOU'LL BE ON THE SAME FLIGHT THEY'RE ON, BUT DON'T WORRY-- I'VE BOUGHT YOU A STRONG GLAMOUR. AND BESIDES, THEY'RE NOT ALLOWED TO NOTICE YOU FOR A FEW DAYS AT LEAST.
YOU CAN'T BRING A GUN ON THE FLIGHT--EVEN IN CHECKED BAGGAGE-- SO YOU'LL HAVE TO BUY ONE AT YOUR FINAL DESTINATION.
AND WHEN DO I KILL THEM?
NOT UNTIL THEY'RE WELL AWAY FROM CIVILIZATION.
MAKE SURE THE BODIES WILL NEVER BE FOUND.
AND GOLDILOCKS-- THIS TIME DON'T BOTCH THE JOB.
NEXT: FINAL DESTINATION!

Cover art by James Jean

NO SHIT? THEY RAN OFF TOGETHER? SNOW WHITE AND THE SHERIFF?
YUP. DAY BEFORE YESTERDAY. ALL OF A SUDDEN, TOO.
SURE, I HEARD THEY WERE--YOU KNOW--SECRETLY BUMPING HEADBOARDS FOR MORE THAN A YEAR NOW, BUT--
YEAH, EVER SINCE SHE GOT OUT OF THE HOSPITAL.
LAUNDROMAT
COMIC NOOK
NEW COMICS EVERY WEDNESDAY
NO, EVEN BEFORE THAT. SINCE REMEMBRANCE DAY--NOT THE LAST ONE, BUT THE YEAR BEFORE--BACK WHEN ROSE RED TURNED UP NOT DEAD.
I HEARD THEY ELOPED.
BIGBY I COULD ALMOST UNDERSTAND, GIVING IN TO HIS ANIMAL URGES, BUT MISS WHITE? SHE'S SUCH AN ICE QUEEN.
ICE CREAM? YUM.
ARE YOU KIDDING? SHE'S GORGEOUS.
I'D SELL MY SOUL FOR ONE NIGHT WITH HER.
OKAY, MAYBE NOT MY SOUL, BUT I'D DEFINITELY SELL YOURS.
ANYONE ELSE HUNGRY?
REDHOOD

Into the Woods

Bill Willingham
writer/creator

Mark Buckingham
penciller

Steve Leialoha
inker

Daniel Vozzo
color/separations

Todd Klein
lettering

Mariah Huehner
assistant editor

James Jean
cover art

Shelly Bond
editor

HMMMN?
WHAT THE HELL?

WHUP
WHUP
WHUP
WHUP
WHUP
HUH?
WHUP
WHUP
WHUP
WHAT ARE YOU DOING, BIGBY?
TIME TO WAKE UP, SNOW. WE'VE GOT PROBLEMS.
PISS, WASH UP AND GET DRESSED-- WHATEVER YOUR MORNING ROUTINE IS. WE NEED TO GET GOING, PRONTO.
WHERE ARE WE, AND WHY AM I IN A TENT?
I DON'T KNOW--
--BUT IT LOOKS LIKE WE'VE BEEN CAMPING HERE FOR TWO OR THREE DAYS.

AT THAT MOMENT, MOST OF A CONTINENT AWAY...
STEP ASIDE. I'M ON OFFICIAL FABLETOWN BUSINESS.
I'M WARNING YOU. WHY WON'T YOU ANSWER ME?
OH DEAR, YOU'RE NOT FABLES!
YOU'RE MUNDY RATS!

I HAD A GOOD LOOK THROUGH OUR EQUIPMENT BEFORE WAKING YOU.
WE'VE BOTH GOT CANCELED ONE-WAY PLANE TICKET STUBS FROM NEW YORK TO SEATTLE, SO MY GUESS IS WE'RE SOMEWHERE IN THE CASCADE MOUNTAINS--BUT IT COULD BE THE OLYMPICS.
ALL OF THIS GEAR IS NEW, AND WAS PURCHASED FROM A SEATTLE OUTFITTER STORE CALLED RECREATIONAL EQUIPMENT. OUR CLOTHES, TOO.
SO WE FLEW OUT HERE WITH NOTHING--NOT EVEN LUGGAGE--AND DECIDED ON A LARK TO GO CAMPING?
TOGETHER?
IT LOOKS THAT WAY.
THAT'S PREPOSTEROUS! I WOULD NEVER DO THAT!
OF COURSE NOT. BUT WE'VE OBVIOUSLY BEEN UNDER SOME SORT OF TRANCE--AN ENCHANTMENT THAT COMPELLED US TO HEAD OUT HERE AND PLAY RANGER RICK.

BUT WE'RE DONE WITH THAT, STARTING RIGHT NOW, SNOW.
LEAVE THIS STUFF BEHIND. WITH A LITTLE LUCK, ANYONE WATCHING US WILL ASSUME WE'RE JUST GOING FOR A STROLL, AND WE'LL BE BACK SHORTLY.
AND JUST WHERE IS IT WE *ARE* GOING?
I FOUND KEYS TO A RENTAL CAR IN YOUR GEAR. IT'LL BE PARKED SOME-WHERE CLOSE BY.
HOW CAN YOU BE SURE OF THAT?

BECAUSE YOU STILL CAN'T *WALK* ALL THAT WELL.
EVEN UNDER A TRANCE, WE WOULDN'T HAVE BEEN ABLE TO PACK ALL THIS *CRAP* VERY FAR FROM OUR TRANS-PORTATION.
AND JUST WHO PUT US UNDER THIS SPELL?
I HAVEN'T A CLUE. BUT EVERY INSTINCT TELLS ME JACK'S BEHIND IT.
IF SO, IT'S LIKELY JUST ONE OF HIS PRANKS AND NOTHING ACTUALLY SINISTER.
THEN WHY ARE WE SUDDENLY RUNNING OFF IN A PANIC?
IN CASE IT ISN'T A HARMLESS PRANK.

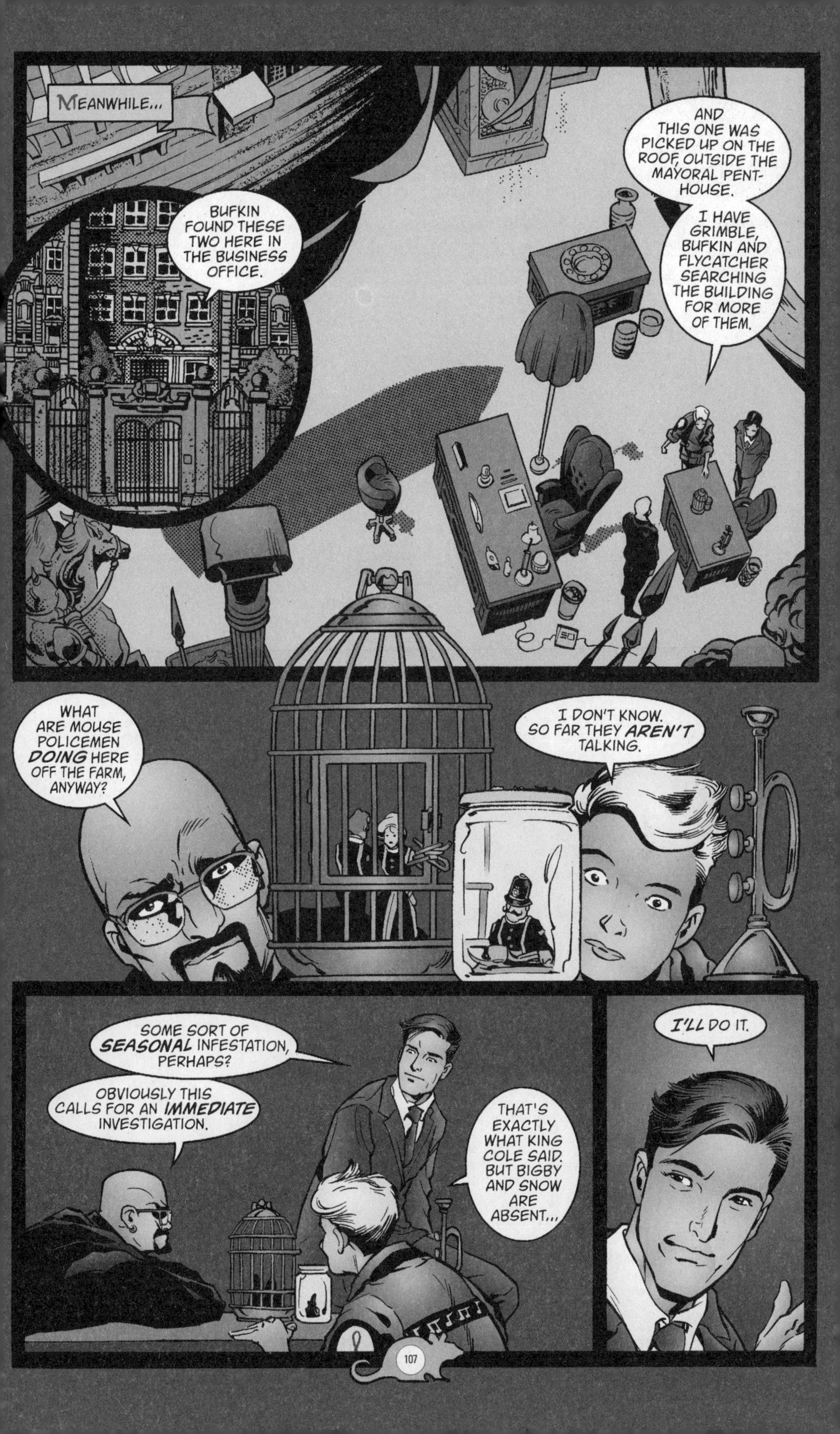
MEANWHILE...
BUFKIN FOUND THESE TWO HERE IN THE BUSINESS OFFICE.
AND THIS ONE WAS PICKED UP ON THE ROOF, OUTSIDE THE MAYORAL PENT-HOUSE.
I HAVE GRIMBLE, BUFKIN AND FLYCATCHER SEARCHING THE BUILDING FOR MORE OF THEM.
WHAT ARE MOUSE POLICEMEN DOING HERE OFF THE FARM, ANYWAY?
I DON'T KNOW. SO FAR THEY AREN'T TALKING.
SOME SORT OF SEASONAL INFESTATION, PERHAPS?
OBVIOUSLY THIS CALLS FOR AN IMMEDIATE INVESTIGATION.
THAT'S EXACTLY WHAT KING COLE SAID. BUT BIGBY AND SNOW ARE ABSENT...
I'LL DO IT.

WHY YOU? THIS DUTY REQUIRES SOMEONE WITH PROVEN STATUS IN THE COMMUNITY--
--SOMEONE MORE INVESTED IN OUR LONG-TERM PROSPERITY.
IT'S HARDLY A JOB WE CAN TRUST TO A NEWLY ARRIVED COMMONER.
NOW WAIT A MINUTE, BLUEBEARD, WE CAN ARGUE MY OTHER MERITS, BUT I AM A PRINCE AGAIN.
I BOUGHT MY TITLE BACK FROM JACK, THE DAY AFTER HE WON THE ONLINE AUCTION.
SNOW WHITE
—DIRECTOR OF OPERATIONS—
HOWEVER...
THAT MAY BE TECHNICALLY TRUE, BUT ONCE A TITLE HAS BEEN BOUGHT AND SOLD A FEW TIMES, LIKE SOME COMMODITY, IT LOSES ITS CACHET.
UHM...BE THAT AS IT MAY, SINCE THIS INVESTIGATION WILL INVOLVE CLOSE COORDINATION WITH THE FARM, AND SINCE PRINCE CHARMING SUCCESSFULLY CONDUCTED THE WAR CRIME TRIALS UP THERE, KING COLE WANTS HIM TO HANDLE IT.
THIS IS A GRIEVOUS MISTAKE. HE'LL LET YOU DOWN. SOONER OR LATER HE LETS EVERYONE DOWN.

HERE WE ARE.
FINALLY. MY LEGS WERE ABOUT TO GIVE OUT. I NEED TO REST.
NOT FOR TOO LONG, SNOW.
I'M LIKING THIS SITUATION LESS AND LESS EVERY MINUTE. WE SHOULD GET OUT OF HERE AS QUICKLY AS POSSIBLE.
THEN YOU DRIVE.
I DON'T KNOW HOW.
THEN LEARN. IT'S HIGH TIME YOU JOINED THE REST OF US IN THE 20TH CENTURY, BIGBY.
IT'S THE 21ST CENTURY NOW.
OH YEAH, I FORGOT. THEY GO BY SO FAST.

BLOWOUT!
BLAM!
HANG ON!
OH GOD!
OH GOD!
OH GOD!
HOLD ON, SNOW! YOU CAN STILL SAVE US, IF YOU CAN KEEP CONTROL OF THE CAR!
YOU CAN DO IT!

YOU'RE DOING FINE! WE'LL MAKE IT YET! AIM FOR THE THICKEST BRUSH!
TRY TO AVOID HITTING THE TREES HEAD ON, BUT USE CONTACT WITH THEM TO SLOW US DOWN!
WE'VE HAD IT NOW!

HONEY, I'M HOME.
THAT'S STILL HILARIOUS EVERY TIME YOU SAY IT.
DON'T GET UP. I HAVE SOME WORK TO DO IN MY DEN.
I DON'T LIKE YOU KEEPING A SECRET LOCKED ROOM IN MY APARTMENT. I DON'T RECALL AGREEING TO LET YOU HAVE AN EXTRA ROOM WHEN I ALLOWED YOU TO MOVE IN HERE.
MY CHARITY TOWARDS HOMELESS EX-HUSBANDS HAS ITS LIMITS.
NOW NOW, BRIAR, DEAR, A GENTLEMAN DOES NEED HIS PRIVACY.
I'LL BE OUT LATER TO RUN YOUR ERRANDS, PRINCESS.
SLAM

NOW THAT WE'RE AWAY FROM PRYING EYES AND EARS, PERHAPS YOU THREE CAN EXPLAIN WHY YOU WERE SO INEPT AS TO GET CAUGHT.
IT WASN'T OUR FAULT, NOBLE PRINCE.
YOU DIDN'T BRING ENOUGH OF US DOWN HERE TO BE ABLE TO GATHER UP ALL THE INFORMATION YOU NEED. WE'RE OVERWORKED.
WE HAD TO TAKE CHANCES TO KEEP TO YOUR SCHEDULE.
COULD YOU SPEAK UP? I CAN BARELY HEAR YOU. WHAT HAPPENED TO SERGEANT WILFRED?
HE HASN'T REPORTED IN FOR DAYS. I'M BEGINNING TO GET WORRIED.
I'M NOT. HE AND CORPORAL REX ARE AMONG THE BEST OF US.
YOU THREE GET SOME REST. NO MORE JOBS FOR A WHILE. WE'LL NEED TO CURTAIL ACTIVITY, NOW THAT THEY'VE DISCOVERED YOU.
I NEED TO THINK ABOUT OUR NEXT MOVE.

SNOW?
SNOW, ARE YOU OKAY?
WAKE UP.
ARE WE ALIVE?
MORE OR LESS. LUCKY US. THE CAR SEEMS TO HAVE ABSORBED MOST OF THE DAMAGE.
LUCKY, HELL. THANK THE MUNDYS AND THEIR MARVELS OF MODERN ENGINEERING. THEY DESIGN THEM NOW TO TAKE ALL THE DAMAGE.
AT LEAST I SEEM TO BE IN ONE PIECE.
ME TOO, EXCEPT FOR THIS.
OH MY GOD. THAT'S A NASTY BREAK. DOES IT--?
IT'LL BE FINE IN A MOMENT.
IT'LL HEAL ITSELF AS SOON AS I CHANGE TO WOLF FORM--PROVIDED I SET THE BONE FIRST.
I'LL NEED YOUR HELP.

PREPARE YOURSELF. IT WON'T BE FUN, SNOW, BUT YOU'VE GOT TO **HARDEN** YOUR HEART TO EVERYTHING BUT GETTING THE JOB DONE.
PULL STEADILY. NO JERKING PLEASE, AND ONCE YOU START, DON'T STOP UNTIL IT'S IN PLACE, EVEN IF I'M SCREAMING BLOODY MURDER. I'LL TRY TO AVOID THRASHING, AT LEAST.
READY?
I THINK SO.
AWWWWOOOOOLL!
THAT DID IT, I THINK. YOU CAN LET GO NOW.
THANK YOU.
LET ME REST A MOMENT, THEN WE'LL BE ON OUR WAY.

YOU'RE BADLY INJURED. WE SHOULDN'T BE GOING ANYWHERE FOR A LONG WHILE.
AND YET WE HAVE TO. WE NEED TO PUT MORE DISTANCE BETWEEN US AND THE GUNMAN.
WHAT GUNMAN?
IT WASN'T JUST A FLAT TIRE THAT SENT US OVER THE CLIFF. THERE WAS A GUNSHOT, BUT ITS SOUND CAME AFTER THE BLOWOUT.
YOU NO DOUBT COULDN'T HEAR IT OVER YOUR OWN SCREAMING AT THE TIME. MY EARS ARE MORE SENSI-TIVE, THOUGH.
THE TRIP DOWN THE CLIFF ACTUALLY HELPED US SOME. IT ABRUPTLY REMOVED US FROM HIS KILLING ZONE-- SAVED US FROM A SECOND SHOT.
BUT THAT WAS SOME TIME AGO, AND HE--WHOEVER THE HUNTER IS--WILL HAVE BEEN MOVING BACK IN ON US FOR ALL THAT TIME.
SO WE'LL NEED TO MOVE OUT FAST, AS SOON AS I CHANGE TO WOLF FORM. NIGHT OR DAY, I CAN COVER A LOT OF MILES QUICKLY, EVEN WITH A PASSENGER.
NOW HELP ME GET UNDRESSED. YOU'LL HAVE TO CARRY WHAT'S LEFT OF MY CLOTHES, AS WELL AS YOUR STUFF, IF YOU WANT ME TO HAVE SOMETHING TO WEAR, ONCE I CHANGE BACK.

WOW!
HANG ON TIGHT, SNOW. YOU CAN'T POSSIBLY HURT ME.

HELLO?
YES, IT'S GOOD NEWS. THE JOB'S FINALLY DONE. I BLASTED THEIR CAR OVER A CLIFF JUST UNDER TWO HOURS AGO.
NO, I COULDN'T HELP LETTING THEM REACH THEIR CAR. IT TOOK ME TWO FUCKING DAYS TO FIND SOMEONE WHO'D SELL ME A RIFLE WITHOUT THE THREE-FUCKING-DAY WAITING PERIOD.
JUST THIS AFTERNOON I GOT UP TO THEIR CAMPSITE, BUT THEY'D ALREADY LEFT.
BEAR III
WELL, IT'S CERTAINLY NOT MY FAULT. IF YOU'D USED A LONGER-LASTING SPELL, THEY'D STILL BE THERE WAITING FOR ME TO WALK UP AND SHOOT THEM AT CLOSE RANGE.
YES, I'LL WORK MY WAY DOWN TO THEIR CRASH SITE TO MAKE SURE THEY'RE DEAD. I WAS ALREADY DOING THAT WHEN YOU CALLED.
NOW HANG UP AND LET ME DO MY WORK.

AND IN FABLE-TOWN...

OHHHHH.

OH MY GOD!
QUIET. I NEED TO GET A FEW HOURS' SLEEP, WHILE IT'S STILL DARK ENOUGH TO CONCEAL US. YOU DO, TOO.
BUT I JUST REALIZED SOMETHING, WOLF. THERE WAS ONLY ONE TENT AND ONE SLEEPING BAG.
SO?
WERE WE *SLEEPING* TOGETHER?
I DOUBT IT. I DON'T THINK I WAS SLEEPING UNDER A TENT AT ALL. I SAW PLENTY OF WOLF TRACKS IN THE CAMPSITE AREA--TRACKS MY SIZE.
APPARENTLY I'D BEEN ASSUMING WOLF FORM AND RUNNING WILD--PROBABLY SLEEPING WILD, TOO. DON'T LET IT BOTHER YOU, PRINCESS. WE'VE GOT OTHER THINGS TO WORRY ABOUT JUST NOW.
IT'S NOT *MY* FAULT IF I'M OVERLY CONCERNED ABOUT WHAT *MIGHT* HAVE HAPPENED BETWEEN US, UNDER THIS SPELL. YOU *CAUSED* IT.

YOU'RE THE ONE WHO CONFESSED AN INTEREST IN ME.
AFTER WHICH YOU PROMPTLY SHOT ME DOWN. NOW CAN WE GET SOME SLEEP?
WHY?
BECAUSE I'M TIRED AND WE HAVE A LONG ROAD AHEAD OF US TOMORROW.
NO, WHAT I MEANT WAS, WHY ME? WHY THE INTEREST?
NOW YOU'RE SUDDENLY IN THE MOOD TO TALK ABOUT THIS? YOUR TIMING AMAZES ME.
I CAN'T SLEEP. I THINK I'M STILL TOO WIRED BY TODAY'S EVENTS. SO WHY AFTER SEVERAL HUNDRED YEARS ARE YOU SUDDENLY ATTRACTED TO ME?
IT'S NOT ALL OF A SUDDEN. I DON'T ACT IMPULSIVELY. YOU SHOULD KNOW THAT BY NOW.
YOU'RE STALLING.
NO, I'M ANSWERING YOUR QUESTION, BUT IN MY OWN WAY. NOW SHUT UP, IF YOU WANT TO HEAR THIS.
NEXT: The Wolf's Tale

Cover art by James Jean

IN THE FOOTHILLS OF THE CASCADE MOUNTAINS...
AMONG MY PEOPLE-- WELL, WHAT USED TO BE MY PEOPLE, AND THEN JUST ON MY MOTHER'S SIDE--THE FIRST STIRRINGS OF ROMANCE ARE USUALLY TRIGGERED WHEN WE ENCOUNTER THE ONE WHO, FOR SOME REASON, JUST SMELLS RIGHT TO US--WHO STANDS OUT FROM EVERYONE ELSE.
ONE OF THE REASONS YOU SURVIVED OUR FIRST MEETING WAS THAT YOUR SCENT SEEMED IMMEDIATELY PLEASING TO ME.
ARE YOU KIDDING ME? I WAS A MESS BACK THEN, AFTER WEEKS ON THE RUN FROM THE ADVERSARY'S LEGIONS, THEN THREE DAYS IN ONE OF HIS CHAIN GANGS. I WAS COVERED WITH DIRT AND HADN'T SEEN A BATH, OR THE WORKING END OF A PERFUME BOTTLE FOR...
NEVERTHELESS.
BUT I WASN'T MUCH INTERESTED IN HUMAN GIRLS BACK THEN. I GUESS IT TOOK CENTURIES OF LIVING AS A HUMAN MYSELF FOR THE ATTRACTION TO GROW ON ME.
SO I'M YOUR FIRST EXPERIMENT WITH AN ACQUIRED TASTE?
NOT EXACTLY.
DUEL
Storybook Love
Part Three
Bill Willingham writer/creator
Mark Buckingham penciller
Steve Leialoha inker
James Jean cover art
Daniel Vozzo color/separations
Todd Klein lettering
Mariah Huehner assistant editor
Shelly Bond editor

YOU'RE THE WOMAN I CAN'T IGNORE.
WHAT DOES THAT MEAN? IT SOUNDS VAGUELY INSULTING.
LIVING IN THE CITY, I HAVE TO SMOKE LIKE A BRISTOL CHIMNEY JUST TO DEADEN MY SENSES ENOUGH TO PUT UP WITH THE MASSIVE INFORMATION OVER-LOAD.
I'VE NOTICED.
AND EVEN WITH THAT, I HAVE TO WORK HARD TO MENTALLY FILTER OUT ALL OF THE MILLIONS OF INTRUSIVE SOUNDS AND SCENTS--EVERY SMOKE-BELCHING VEHICLE, EVERY SINGLE PERSON, WITH THEIR NATURAL SMELLS, PLUS THE DIFFERENT COLOGNES AND PERFUMES THEY DRENCH THEM-SELVES IN.
EVERY MORSEL OF FOOD SERVED IN TWENTY THOUSAND HOMES AND RESTAURANTS, AND EVERY SCRAP OF GARBAGE THEY PRODUCE.
I'D GO CRAZY IF I COULDN'T BLOCK IT ALL OUT.
AND WHAT DOES THIS HAVE TO DO WITH ME, BIGBY?
BECAUSE YOU AND YOU ALONE I CAN'T BLOCK OUT, NO MATTER HOW HARD I TRY--AND BELIEVE ME, I'VE TRIED.

I KNOW WHERE YOU ARE, EVERY SECOND OF EVERY DAY. I KNOW IF YOU'RE HAVING GOOD OR BAD DREAMS WHILE YOU SLEEP.
I KNOW WHAT KIND OF MOOD YOU'RE IN BY SUBTLE CHANGES IN YOUR NATURAL MUSK, NO MATTER HOW MUCH YOU BATHE...
...OR WHAT MANUFACTURED SCENTS YOU CHOOSE TO WEAR.
I KNOW WHEN YOU'RE HAPPY, WHICH IS RARE; WHEN YOU'RE SAD; AND WHEN YOU FEEL DESPERATELY LONELY--WHICH IS ALL TOO OFTEN.
I THINK WE SHOULD STOP TALKING ABOUT THIS NOW.
I KNOW YOU GET JEALOUS WHENEVER YOU HAVE TO TALK TO BEAUTY, BECAUSE OF HOW SUCCESSFUL HER MARRIAGE HAS BEEN, ALL THINGS CONSIDERED--HOW UNRELENTINGLY LOYAL BEAST IS TO HER.
PLEASE--
AND YOU FEEL GUILTY FOR RESENTING HER HAPPINESS, AND HOW THAT MAKES YOU SNAP AT HER, EVEN THOUGH IT'S NOT HER YOU'RE ANGRY WITH.
STOP IT. THIS IS--IT'S TOO CREEPY--LIKE YOU'VE BEEN STALKING ME FOR ALL THESE YEARS.
I'D STOP IT IF I COULD.
YOU'LL RECALL, IN THE FIRST YEARS IN EXILE, I TRIED TO LIVE APART FROM YOU AND THE OTHER FABLES. BUT YOU INSISTED I COME TO THE NEW WORLD AND JOIN YOUR GRAND EXPERIMENT.
STILL...
YOU SHOULD LEARN NOT TO ASK QUESTIONS YOU CAN'T STAND TO HEAR THE ANSWERS TO.

WHERE'S MY BREAKFAST?
WHERE ARE YOU FOR THAT MATTER?
THIS ISN'T AT ALL LIKE YOU.
HOBBES?
YOUR BUTLER ISN'T HERE, BLUEBEARD. I SENT HIM AWAY--GAVE HIM THE DAY OFF, IF YOU WILL.
WE'RE ALONE, WITH NO ONE TO INTERRUPT OUR BUSINESS TOGETHER.
WHAT BUSINESS WOULD THAT BE, PRINCE CHARMING?
SWORDS AT DAWN, DREAD LORD.
ISN'T THAT HOW THESE THINGS ARE TRADITIONALLY DONE?
WHAT THINGS? ARE YOU INSANE? THIS IS NONSENSE!

DON'T TRY TO LEAVE THIS ROOM, OR I'LL RUN YOU THROUGH. DON'T TRY TO GRAB UP SOME HIDDEN GUN, OR OTHER WEAPON OF ADVANTAGE, OR I'LL RUN YOU THROUGH.
STOP TALKING LIKE THAT!
YOUR ONLY CHANCE TO SURVIVE THE NEXT FEW MINUTES IS TO TAKE UP A BLADE AND KILL ME, FOR I CERTAINLY INTEND TO KILL YOU.
BUT WHY? WHAT HAVE I DONE?
THERE ARE SO MANY GOOD REASONS TO END YOUR MISERABLE EXISTENCE, IT'S HARD TO CHOOSE.
BUT, ALL OTHER THINGS CONSIDERED, I SUPPOSE I'M GOING TO KILL YOU AS A FAVOR TO SNOW. I'VE TREATED HER SO BADLY OVER THE YEARS THAT IT'S HIGH TIME TO DO SOMETHING TO MAKE UP FOR IT.
BY KILLING ME? WHAT WILL THAT ACCOMPLISH? I'VE NEVER DONE ANYTHING TO HER!
DON'T DISSEMBLE. I'VE HAD A LOOK AT YOUR DIARY--WELL, NOT DIRECTLY, BUT MY SPY REPORTED IN. I KNOW YOU'RE PLANNING TO MURDER BIGBY.

AND FOR REASONS THAT DEFY UNDERSTANDING, SNOW SEEMS TO LIKE THE MANGY BEAST--HELL, SHE MIGHT ACTUALLY BE IN LOVE WITH HIM.
BUT--?
OH, DON'T GO BY HOW SHE TREATS HIM. SHE'S BEEN SO RELENTLESSLY BETRAYED BY EVERYONE SHE'S EVER LOVED, SHE CAN'T HELP BUT SNAP AND SNARL AT A NEW LOVE.
REMEMBER, I'VE TAKEN MY TURN ON THE RECEIVING END OF HER AFFECTIONS. IT'S A LOT LIKE BEING IN A KNIFE FIGHT.
I WAS FAR FROM THE WORST OF THE LOT--YOU SHOULD HAVE SEEN HER STEPMOTHER--BUT MY BETRAYAL SEEMED TO HAVE BEEN THE PROVERBIAL LAST STRAW. IT DOESN'T OFTEN SHOW, BUT I DO REGRET THAT.
BUT WHATEVER THE REASON, SHE SEEMS TO WANT THE OLD DOG, SO, EVEN THOUGH I FIND HIM PERSONALLY DISTASTEFUL, I CAN'T ALLOW YOU TO KILL HIM.
SINCE WHEN DOES AN UNREPENTANT ROGUE LIKE YOU SUDDENLY DECIDE TO ACT SO NOBLY? HOW DO YOU NOT CHOKE ON SUCH HYPOCRISY?
LOOK AT IT THIS WAY: WITH SOMEONE LIKE ME, NOBLE URGES OCCUR SO SELDOM THAT I CAN HARDLY AFFORD TO IGNORE THE RARE FEW THAT DO COME ALONG.

NOW, I THINK YOU'VE KEPT ME TALKING MERELY TO STALL FOR TIME. FILL YOUR HAND, BLUEBEARD, AND LET'S BE ABOUT OUR GRIM BUSINESS.
FINE! I'LL RUN YOU THROUGH, IF YOU INSIST!
I DO.
REMEMBER HOW EASILY I BEAT YOU IN OUR RECENT FENCING BOUT?
PERFECTLY. BUT LET'S SEE IF REAL BLADES AND REAL DANGER MAKE A DIFFERENCE THIS TIME, SHALL WE?
LAY ON, THEN!

I'M TIRED, BIGBY. MY LEGS ARE ABOUT TO GIVE OUT.
IF YOU'D TURN BACK INTO A WOLF, I COULD RIDE AGAIN AND WE'D COVER MORE GROUND.
SOON, BUT NOT YET.
TRY TO HOLD ON FOR A BIT LONGER. WE DON'T WANT TO GET TOO FAR AHEAD OF OUR PURSUER.
WHY NOT? ISN'T THAT THE WHOLE POINT OF GETTING AWAY?
NOT ALWAYS. IF WE SIMPLY RUN FOR IT, WE COULD LIKELY GET AWAY THIS TIME, BUT AT THE RISK OF LETTING HER CHOOSE WHEN AND WHERE TO STRIKE THE NEXT TIME.
BETTER TO FIND GOOD GROUND HERE AND END IT.
"HER"?
DID YOU SAY "HER"?
YEAH, I FINALLY GOT A WHIFF OF OUR ENEMY. SHE'S DEFINITELY FEMALE AND PROBABLY A FABLE. DO YOU HEAR THAT SOUND--FAINT BUT GETTING CLOSER?
THE CHAIN SAW? YOU SAID THIS IS LOGGING COUNTRY.

SIMILAR SOUND, BUT IT'S NOT A CHAIN SAW. MY GUESS IS A MOTOR BIKE.
SHE'S CLOSING IN, BUT WE MIGHT FINALLY HAVE THE PLACE HERE TO GIVE HER A PROPER WELCOME.
YOU KNOW WHO IT IS, DON'T YOU? IT'S GOT TO BE GOLDILOCKS!
THAT WOULD BE MY GUESS. UNLESS YOU'RE AWARE OF OTHER FUGITIVE, GUN-HAPPY, HOMICIDAL, FEMALE FABLES WITH A SPECIAL NUT AGAINST YOU?
SEE HOW FAR YOU CAN CRAWL UNDER THOSE BOULDERS. YOU'LL NEED SAFE SHELTER FOR THIS NEXT PART.
WHAT ARE YOU GOING TO DO?
A TALENT I GOT FROM MY DAD'S SIDE OF THE FAMILY--ONE I HAVEN'T HAD THE NEED TO USE IN A GOODLY WHILE.
IT'S TIME FOR A BIT OF THE OLD HUFF AND PUFF.

OW!
I'VE GOT YOU NOW, PRINCE OF CORPSES!
NO MERCY!
NONE NEEDED.

BUSINESS
OFFICE
S. WHITE

RIIIING
RIIING
RIIIING

RIIING
RIIIING
RIIIING
RIIING
?
SNOW WHITE
DIRECT OF OPERATIONS
HELLO?
BUSINESS OFFICE.

NO, SNOW WHITE'S NOT HERE. SHE LEFT TOWN.

NO, BIGBY LEFT TOWN TOO.

NO, KING COLE NEVER COMES DOWN HERE.

NO, BLUE BOY'S FAST ASLEEP.

WHO'S IN CHARGE?

I GUESS I AM.
I RUN FABLE-TOWN NOW.

WHY NOT? I'M A GOOD MONKEY!

I HARDLY EVER THROW MY POOP ANYMORE.

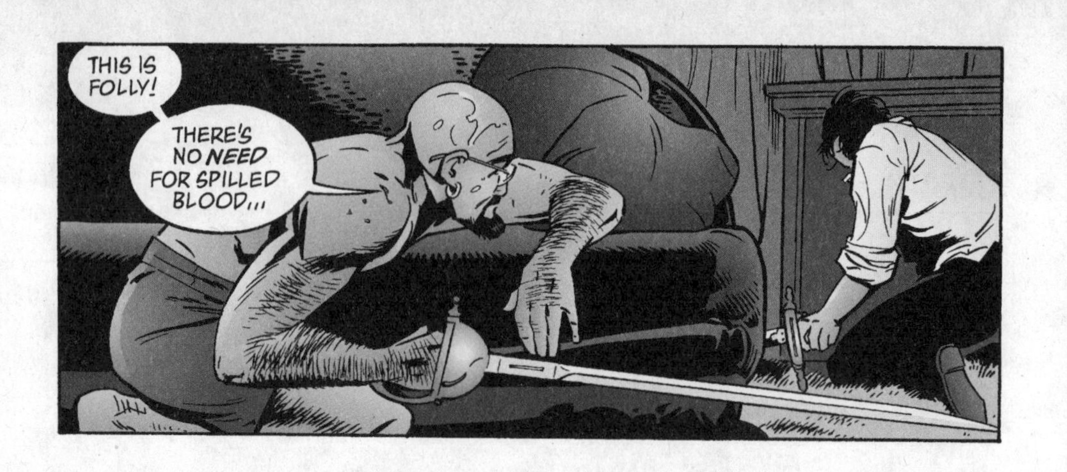
THIS IS FOLLY!
THERE'S NO NEED FOR SPILLED BLOOD...

...WHEN SPILLED GOLD HAS SO MUCH MORE LUSTER TO IT!
LEAVE OFF NOW AND I'LL SHOWER YOU WITH AS MUCH AS YOU CAN CARRY!
SILLY MAN! YOU'RE NOT VERY QUICK ON THE UPTAKE, ARE YOU?
I INTEND TO HAVE ALL YOUR RICHES -- AS SOON AS YOU'RE OUT OF THE WAY.
NOBLE IMPULSES ONLY GO SO FAR.

BIGBY?
WHERE DID YOU GO? ARE YOU DOING THIS?

WHAT THE FUCK?!!

WE HAVE TO STOP THIS!
WE WILL SOON.
NO, YOU DON'T UNDERSTAND!
YOU CAN'T SAVE BIGBY THIS WAY! I'VE ALREADY--
WILL YOU PLEASE SHUT UP?
TRY TO DIE WITH JUST A LITTLE DIGNITY.

BIGBY?
IS IT OVER?

YES, IT'S SAFE TO COME OUT NOW.
I'M DONE.
THAT WAS--
HOW DID YOU--
LIKE I SAID--BLAME MY *DAD*.
I GUESS I NEVER MENTIONED BEFORE THAT I'M THE PRODUCT OF A *MIXED MARRIAGE*.

MY FATHER WAS THE NORTH WIND--
--AND *HOW* HE MET MY MOTHER AND TOOK A *SPARK* TO HER--WELL, THAT'S A LONG AND INTERESTING STORY FOR ANOTHER TIME.

LIKE EVERYONE ELSE, I HEARD THE STORY ABOUT YOU AND THE THREE PIGS, BUT I NEVER IMAGINED WHAT YOU COULD REALLY DO.
AND I WAS STILL JUST A GROWING PUP BACK THEN. I DOUBT EVEN A BRICK HOUSE COULD SURVIVE NOW.
DID YOU GET HER?
IS GOLDILOCKS DEAD?
NO, UN-FORTUNATELY-- BUT NOT FOR LACK OF TRYING.
KILLING HER THIS WAY WAS A LONG SHOT. IT WASN'T MY PRIMARY GOAL.
I'VE SUCCEEDED IN THE TWO THINGS I'D HOPED TO ACCOMPLISH.
WHICH ARE...?
FIRST, I'VE JUST CREATED A TRAIL POINTING TO US THAT AN IDIOT COULDN'T MISS. GOLDI-LOCKS SHOULD HAVE NO TROUBLE FINDING US NOW.

AND, MORE IMPORTANT, I'VE JUST SHOWN THE LOCAL WINDS WHO'S BOSS.
THEY'RE OBEYING ME NOW--FOR A WHILE AT LEAST.
LONG ENOUGH THAT THEY'LL MANEUVER TO KEEP GOLDILOCKS UPWIND OF US AT ALL TIMES--CARRYING HER SCENT DIRECTLY TO ME, NO MATTER WHAT PATH SHE TAKES.
NOW I'LL KNOW WHERE SHE IS EVERY SECOND, RIGHT UP UNTIL THE MOMENT SHE ARRIVES.
SO THIS TIME WE'VE SET A TRAP FOR HER?
YUP.
HIDING, STAYING QUIET AND STAYING OUT OF MY WAY--
AND WHAT'S MY PART?
--IF THINGS GO ACCORDING TO PLAN.
JUST IN CASE, THOUGH, LET'S TALK ABOUT WHAT YOU SHOULD BE PREPARED TO DO IF THINGS DON'T TURN OUT THE WAY I EXPECT.

THAT'S IT!
I SURRENDER!
YOU WIN!
YOU HAVEN'T BEEN LISTENING.
BUT I'M BEGGING YOU!
SURRENDER ISN'T AN OPTION!
AAAHH!
YOU PRICK! YOU'VE KILLED ME!
BUT I WIN TOO, THOUGH-- IN A WAY.
I WAS TRYING TO TELL YOU--BUT YOU WOULDN'T LISTEN.
YOU SEE--I ALREADY KILLED THE WOLF, AND YOUR PRINCESS, TOO.
ALREADY DONE.

OH MY.
YOU MIGHT AS WELL SHOW YOURSELVES.
I KNOW YOU'RE NEAR.

AS YOU WISH.
NEXT:
GETTING AWAY WITH MURDER

Cover art by James Jean

BLAM!
ROAD-RUNNER AND COYOTE UGLY
Storybook Love
Part Four
Bill Willingham writer/creator
Mark Buckingham penciller
Steve Leialoha inker
Daniel Vozzo color/separations
Todd Klein lettering
James Jean cover art
Mariah Huehner assistant editor
Shelly Bond editor

BLAM!
BLAM!
NOW, WHERE ARE YOU HIDING, LITTLE PRINCESS?
COME OUT, COME OUT, WHEREVER YOU ARE!

YOU...SHOULD... HAVE...USED... SILVER.
WHAT'S THAT?
EXCUSE ME?
SILVER BULLETS. THESE STEEL AND LEAD THINGS HURT LIKE THE DICKENS, BUT THEY CAN'T KILL ME OR DO ANYTHING PERMANENT.
WELL, THAT'S NO FAIR. I'M USING TOP OF THE LINE 30-378 WEATHERBY HUNTING ROUNDS. THEY CAN KILL A CHARGING ELEPHANT WITH ONE SHOT AND THEY SHOULD HAVE MADE A RIGHT ROYAL PUDDING OF YOUR INNARDS.
MY BONES AND VESSELS AND GUTS ARE ALREADY KNITTING BACK TOGETHER. I'LL HAVE YOU BETWEEN MY JAWS SOON ENOUGH.
DO TELL?
THEN HERE'S AN APPETIZER.
BLAM!

I'M FAR FROM IGNORANT, WOLF. IF I RECALL MY WEREWOLF LORE CORRECTLY, SILVER'S NOT THE ONLY THING THAT CAN DESTROY YOU.
FIRE WORKS TOO, RIGHT?
SO I'LL BUILD A NICE BONFIRE--WITH YOU IN THE CENTER OF IT.
PAUSING, OF COURSE, TO PUT THE OCCASIONAL ROUND IN YOU, TO KEEP YOU NICE AND HELPLESS WHILE I WORK.
HOW'S THAT?

HOW'S THIS!

WHAT DID--?
I FELL DOWN.
I THINK I--
OH GOD!
OH GOD!

DID I DROP MY GLASSES?
WHY DO I FEEL SO--
--SNOW! THERE YOU ARE!
WHY'S MY HAIR WET?
DID YOU DO THIS?
WHAT... DID...YOU... DO?

--AARUPP--
FALL BACK DOWN! WHY AREN'T YOU DEAD?
MY RIFLE.

GOLDY'S GOT YOU NOW, SNOW.

SHOOT YOU NOW-- UUURRGL

NO, NOT NOW!
NEVER AGAIN!

FALL *DOWN!*
--NOT THE BOSS OF ME!
--STILL STANDING, *BITCH.* NYAH, NYAH.

...OOPS...

SEE?

SEE?

--CAN TAKE ANYTHING YOU CAN DISH OUT.

DID SHE GO OVER THE CLIFF?
BIGBY!

ARE YOU OKAY?
NOT BY A LONG SHOT, BUT I'M GETTING THERE. WHAT ABOUT GOLDILOCKS, THOUGH? IS SHE DEAD THIS TIME?

YES. DEFINITELY.
I HOPE SO. SHE'S A POPULAR FABLE WITH THE MUNDYS. THEY WON'T LET HER DIE EASILY.

WHAT DO WE DO NOW?
SLEEP-- FOR ABOUT TWELVE HOURS.
THEN WE GO HOME.

THE NEXT DAY...
GOOD MORNING, MISS MUFFET.
Web 'n' Muffet MARKET
HOW ARE YOU ON THIS GLORIOUS DAY?
IT'S MRS. WEB NOW.
IS IT? FORGIVE ME, BUT I'VE STILL GOT SO MUCH LOCAL NEWS AND GOSSIP TO CATCH UP ON. BELATED CONGRATULATIONS.
WHAT'S THAT YOU'VE GOT THERE?
THIS? JUST A DEAD BODY. NOTHING TO WORRY YOURSELF ABOUT.
DO ENJOY THE DAY, MRS. WEB.
Web 'n' Muffet MARKET

MORNING, GRIMBLE. IS THE BUSINESS OFFICE OPEN YET?

HUH?
UH?
YEAH.
HEY, WHAT D'YOU GOT THERE, Y'HIGHNESS?

YOU'D BEST TAG ALONG, IF YOU WANT TO KNOW. I CAN'T KEEP *EXPLAINING* IT OVER AND OVER AGAIN.

USINESS
OFFICE
S.WHITE
RISE AND SHINE, BUCKO.
SORRY I DIDN'T MAKE IT IN YESTERDAY. ANY CRISIS IN MY ABSENCE?

NOPE. ALL'S WELL IN BUFKINTOWN.
EXCUSE ME? WHAT DID YOU SAY?
I CHANGED THE NAME WHILE I WAS IN CHARGE.
GET TO WORK, MONKEY.
GOOD MORNING, BLUE BOY. RING THE MAYOR AND TELL HIM HE'LL WANT TO COME DOWN HERE LICKETY-SPLIT.
NO WAY! KING COLE NEVER COMES DOWN HERE.
WHAT'S THAT?
BLUEBEARD'S CORPSE. I MURDERED HIM YESTERDAY. AND NOW I'M GOING TO DUMP HIM DOWN THE WITCHING WELL TO HIDE THE EVIDENCE.
I SUSPECT KING COLE WILL WANT TO KNOW WHY. CALL HIM. YOU'LL SEE.
I'M NOT SURE YOU SHOULD BE DUMPING BODIES ANYWHERE, Y'GRACE.
POSSIBLY SO, AND YET I INTEND TO DO JUST THAT. COME GIVE ME A HAND, WON'T YOU?
THERE'S A GOOD MAN.

JUST ABOUT AN HOUR LATER...
TERRIBLE THING! MONSTROUS!
NOT REALLY, KING COLE. HE NEEDED KILLING.
DID YOU KNOW HE WAS HOLDING BACK MAGIC ARTIFACTS OF TACTICAL AND STRATEGIC VALUE--IN BLATANT CONTRAVENTION OF FABLETOWN LAW?
SNOW WHITE
HE HAS A BLOODY ARSENAL IN THAT PLACE OF HIS--AND I'VE BARELY BEGUN TO ROOT OUT ALL OF HIS HIDEY-HOLES.
NOT THE POINT! WHAT HAPPENED TO DUE PROCESS? CAN'T JUST TAKE IT UPON YOURSELF TO KILL OUR BIGGEST ANNUAL CONTRIBUTOR!
OH, IS THAT YOUR CONCERN? WELL, I'VE GOT GOOD NEWS FOR YOU, SIR.
NO DOUBT CERTAIN HE'D LIVE FOREVER, BLUEBEARD DIED WITHOUT LEAVING A WILL. THEREFORE, ALL OF HIS RICHES GO DIRECTLY TO FABLETOWN.
THAT IS HOW IT WORKS, ISN'T IT?
REALLY? NO WILL? YOU'RE POSITIVE?

AND HE WAS LOADED--FAR BEYOND ANYONE'S IMAGINATION. YOU NO LONGER HAVE TO BOW AND SCRAPE TO GET HIS PITTANCE OF A HANDOUT EVERY YEAR.
YOU GET IT ALL-- EVERY LAST PENNY-- RIGHT NOW.
WHY, THAT'S-- MARVELOUS!
STILL HAVE TO BE AN OFFICIAL HEARING, OF COURSE. STRICTLY A FORMALITY. BUT BEST TO DO THINGS CORRECTLY.
THEN I SUGGEST WE SHOULD HAVE IT NOW, BEFORE SNOW AND BIGBY RETURN.
YOU KNOW THEY'LL TRY TO DRAG THINGS OUT--NEEDLESSLY COMPLICATING EVERYTHING.
COMING BACK? TRULY? YOU HEARD FROM THEM?
YES SIR, THEY CALLED ABOUT TEN MINUTES AGO. THEY'RE STUCK AT SOME LOGGING CAMP NOW, BUT THEY PLAN TO CATCH A PLANE BACK HERE AS SOON AS POSSIBLE.
TURNING OUT TO BE A GREAT DAY INDEED!
GLORIOUS!
SNOW WHITE
SW

LATER STILL THAT DAY...
WE'D LIKE TO THANK YOU FOR FLYING WITH US THIS EVENING, AND LET US BE THE FIRST TO WELCOME YOU TO NEW YORK'S LAGUARDIA AIRPORT.
FIRST THING I'M GOING TO DO IS SINK INTO A HOT BATH FOR A WEEK.
FIRST THING I'M GOING TO DO IS FIND JACK AND WRING HIS NECK.
BIGBY, BEFORE WE FACE THE OTHERS, WE SHOULD SETTLE ONE THING. ABOUT WHAT YOU SAID TO ME THAT NIGHT...
IF YOU'RE WORRIED THAT I'M GOING TO CONTINUE "STALKING" YOU-- DON'T.

I CAN EASILY MOVE OUT OF THE WOODLAND, IF IT BOTHERS YOU SO MUCH.
NO, THAT'S NOT WHAT I MEANT AND NOT WHAT I WANT.
WE HAD TO RELY ON EACH OTHER OUT THERE, FOR OUR VERY LIVES, AND WE ENDED UP SAVING EACH OTHER. BY ANY STANDARD, WE'RE CLOSER NOW THAN WE'VE EVER BEEN.
OKAY, NOW I'M CONFUSED. WHAT ARE YOU GETTING AT, SNOW?
I'M NOT THE KIND OF WOMAN TO BE FLATTERED BY SOMEONE WHO TRICKS ME INTO GOING TO A DANCE WITH HIM, BY CLAIMING IT WILL HELP SOLVE MY SISTER'S MURDER.
BUT IF SOME STRAIGHTFORWARD, NICE GUY WERE TO ASK ME OUT TO DINNER OR A MOVIE, SOMETIME NEXT WEEK OR SO--AND HE WAS WILLING TO GO VERY SLOWLY...
WELL, I SURE WOULDN'T MIND A NIGHT OUT AMONG THE MUNDYS ONCE IN A WHILE.
I'LL BE DAMNED.

LIFE GOES ON.
YOU WORK FOR ME NOW, HOBBES, UNLESS OF COURSE, AS A NON-HUMAN FABLE WHOSE GLAMOUR IS ABOUT TO EXPIRE, YOU WOULD PREFER TO MOVE UP TO THE FARM?
I AM DEDICATED TO A LIFE OF SERVICE, SIR, AND YOU ARE A GENTLEMAN OF BREEDING.
GOOD. GLAD TO HEAR IT. WELCOME ABOARD. YOU'VE HITCHED YOUR WAGON TO A RISING STAR THIS TIME.
WHAT ARE YOUR INSTRUCTIONS, SIR?
FIRST, I NEED TO GET MY HANDS ON YOUR FORMER MASTER'S FORTUNES.
HOW IS THAT POSSIBLE, SIR? ISN'T IT COMMUNITY PROPERTY NOW?
YES IT IS, WHICH MEANS I'M JUST GOING TO HAVE TO BECOME THE LEADER OF THE COMMUNITY.
HOW LONG HAS KING COLE BEEN MAYOR--HUNDREDS OF YEARS, RIGHT? SO WHY NO REGULAR ELECTIONS IN ALL THAT TIME?
I THINK I'M BEGINNING TO UNDERSTAND, SIR.
THERE'S YOUR FIRST ASSIGNMENT, THEN. YOU'VE GOT LIBRARY PRIVILEGES, RIGHT? GET YOURSELF DOWN TO THE BUSINESS OFFICE AND START RESEARCHING FABLETOWN'S ELECTION LAWS.

NO, NO MEDICATIONS ARE NECESSARY, MISS WHITE. YOU'LL WANT TO EXERCISE EVERY DAY, BUT DON'T OVERDO IT.
OTHER THAN THAT, EAT WHEN YOU'RE HUNGRY, SLEEP WHEN YOU'RE TIRED, AND EAT SODA CRACKERS TO SETTLE YOUR STOMACH.
THANK YOU, DOCTOR SWINEHEART. GOODBYE NOW.
I GUESS CONGRATULATIONS ARE IN ORDER. COME AND SEE ME IN A FEW WEEKS FOR A FOLLOW-UP.
BIGBY? GET YOUR TRAITOROUS ASS UP TO MY APARTMENT IN THE NEXT FIVE MINUTES! I DON'T CARE IF YOU'RE BUSY! MOVE IT OR LOSE IT!

FOUR MINUTES AND FIFTY-FOUR SECONDS LATER...
--THREW UP THIS MORNING, YESTERDAY MORNING, AND THE DAY BEFORE!
OH MY GOD, YOU'RE PREGNANT? I'M GOING TO BE A FATHER?

DON'T YOU DARE BE HAPPY ABOUT THIS! YOU TOLD ME WE DIDN'T DO ANYTHING! YOU SAID YOU SLEPT OUTSIDE!
HOW WOULD I KNOW? I HAVE NO MEMORIES OF THE TIME WE WERE BOTH UNDER THE SPELL! DO YOU? HOW DOES THIS BECOME MY FAULT?

YOU LIED TO ME! YOU'VE GOT ALL THOSE SPECIAL SENSES YOU'RE ALWAYS BOASTING ABOUT, SO YOU WOULD HAVE KNOWN WHAT WE DID AS SOON AS WE CAME TO, BUT YOU HID IT!
MAYBE IT WAS YOU WHO SEDUCED ME! DID YOU CONSIDER THAT?

I TOLD YOU WHAT YOU NEEDED TO HEAR IN ORDER TO STAY CALM AND FOCUSED IN A DANGEROUS SITUATION.

SO WHAT DO WE DO NOW?

PLEASE GO.
I'D LIKE TO BE ALONE.

Cover art by James Jean

ONE BRIGHTLY DAWNING DAY...

...IN THE WOODLAND'S VASTY BUSINESS OFFICE.

A PERFECT DAY FOR A BIT OF EARLY MORNING LARCENY.

AH HAH!
YOU SHOULD HAVE STORED IT ON A HIGHER SHELF, THOUGH THAT STILL WOULDN'T HAVE STOPPED ME.

AND YOU SHOULD MAKE LESS NOISE THE NEXT TIME YOU BREAK INTO MY HOUSE.
YARG!

DIDN'T ANYONE TELL YOU THE WHOLE POINT OF SNEAKING AROUND IS TO BE SNEAKY?

AND HOW WERE YOU PLANNING TO GET THE JAR'S LID OPEN?

LOOKIE HERE!
I CAUGHT ONE, BIGBY! I CAUGHT ONE!

THIS ONE MADE IT ALL THE WAY UP TO THE JAR!
OW!
THIS IS A SMALL ROOM, BUFKIN. YOU PROBABLY DON'T NEED TO SCREECH QUITE SO LOUDLY.

SO, IT'S EDDIE UNDERFOOT--DOWN FROM THE FARM TO MAKE YOUR TRY AT THE BARLEY-CORNS. THE MOUSE POLICE WARNED ME YOU HAD COME OF AGE.
DID THEY? THOSE RATFINKS!
HOW DID YOU GET DOWN HERE, EDDIE?
I HITCHED A RIDE ON THE BACK OF LAST NIGHT'S MESSAGE BIRD.

WELL, YOU'RE GOING BACK THE SAME WAY TODAY. REPORT IN TO THE MPS WHEN YOU GET HOME. AND THEN STAY PUT.
NO FAIR, BIGBY!

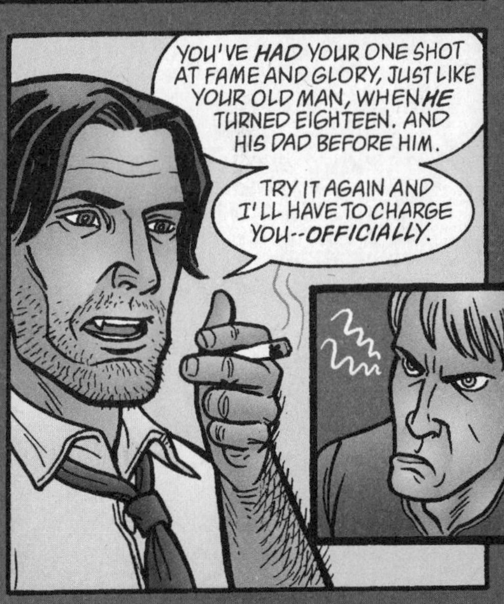
YOU'VE HAD YOUR ONE SHOT AT FAME AND GLORY, JUST LIKE YOUR OLD MAN, WHEN HE TURNED EIGHTEEN. AND HIS DAD BEFORE HIM.
TRY IT AGAIN AND I'LL HAVE TO CHARGE YOU--OFFICIALLY.

OINK!
GET HIM OUT OF HERE, BUFKIN. MAKE SURE HE GOES HOME TODAY.
ROGER DODGER, OLD CODGER!

BIGBY?
HMMM?
I DON'T GET IT. YOU LET THAT KID GO WITH JUST A WARNING?

YEAH. SO WHAT?
YOU CHARGE ME EACH TIME YOU CATCH ME EATING FLIES, WHICH IS ONLY A MINOR OFFENSE, BUT TRYING TO STEAL MAGIC STUFF FROM THE BUSINESS OFFICE IS A GREAT BIG CRIME.

THIS IS A SPECIAL SITUATION. EVERY BOY IN SMALLTOWN TRIES TO STEAL A MAGIC BARLEYCORN ONCE HE COMES OF AGE.
IT'S EXPECTED OF THEM. A TRADITIONAL RITE OF PASSAGE, DATING BACK TO--WELL, IT'S A LONG STORY.

I'VE GOT TIME.

OINK!
WHAT THE HELL, WHY NOT?
PLANT YOURSELF, FLYCATCHER, AND I'LL TELL YOU A TALE.

"LONG AGO, IN THE HOMELANDS, WHEN MOST PEOPLE STILL BELIEVED THEY HAD A CHANCE TO DEFEAT THE ADVERSARY'S INVADING ARMIES, THE KINGDOM OF LILLIPUT WAS AMONG THOSE DETERMINED TO DO THEIR PART.
"SO, THEY MUSTERED UP A VOLUNTEER REGIMENT--DUBBED IT THE FIRST LILLIPUTIAN EXPEDITIONARY AND LIBERATION FORCE--AND MARCHED THEM OFF, AMIDST APPROPRIATE POMP AND FANFARE, TO AID IN THE WAR EFFORT."
BE CAREFUL!
BE SURE TO CHANGE YOUR SOCKS EVERY DAY! AND STAY AWAY FROM FOREIGN GIRLS!
MAKE US PROUD, SON!
BARLEYCORN BRIDES
Bill Willingham: writer-creator
Linda Medley: artist
Todd Klein: letters
Daniel Vozzo: color and seps
James Jean: cover art
Mariah Huehner: asst. ed.
Shelly Bond: editor

"BRAVELY, THEY CROSSED THE WIDE, WILD SEAS, TO DISTANT LANDS THEY'D NEVER BEFORE VISITED.
LAND HO!

"ONLY TO BE GREETED WITH QUITE A SURPRISE ON THEIR ARRIVAL."
OD'S BLOOD!
THIS IS A LAND OF GIANTS!

"A HURRIED MEETING OF THEIR OFFICERS WAS CALLED."
ONE SINGLE SOLDIER IN THIS LAND COULD SQUISH THE LOT OF US UNDER HIS BOOT.
WE CAN'T HELP HERE. TURN THE TROOPS AROUND, CAPTAIN. WE'RE GOING HOME.

"BUT WHEN THEY GOT BACK TO THEIR SHIP, THEY FOUND THAT HOME WAS SUDDENLY A LONG WAY AWAY."
OUR SHIP! SUNK -- AND BURNED!
CAPTURE THAT ENEMY SOLDIER, CAPTAIN. I WANT TO QUESTION HIM.

FINALLY AWAKE? GOOD.
NOW WE CAN TALK.
"COLONEL WUDDERSHANKS QUESTIONED THEIR CAPTIVE FOR HOURS."

OUR SCOUTING PARTY FOUND THE SHIP AND WRECKED IT. MY SERGEANT POSTED ME HERE WHILE THEY WENT OFF TO FIND ITS MINIATURE CREW.
AND HE DISPATCHED A RUNNER TO HEADQUARTERS, TO REPORT THAT SOMEWHERE THERE'S A LAND OF TINY FOLK WHO'LL BE RIDICULOUSLY EASY TO CONQUER. ONE SQUAD OF US COULD DO IT.
CAN I HAVE SOME WATER NOW?
SOON.

"AND MORE HOURS."
WE CAN'T GO HOME AND WE CAN'T STAY HERE. THE OTHER GOBLINS WILL BE BACK SOONER OR LATER.
THEN WE'LL JUST HAVE TO FIND SOMEWHERE ELSE TO GO.
MUSTER THE TROOPS, CAPTAIN.

"AND SO THE LILLIPUTIAN EXPEDITIONARY FORCE BECAME A BAND OF WANDERING REFUGEES, JUST ONE MORE SUCH GROUP IN A STRANGE, GIANT WORLD."
HOW LONG DO YOU THINK IT'LL BE BEFORE WE SEE OUR HOME AGAIN?
YEARS AT LEAST.
MAYBE NEVER. EVEN IF WE HAD A SHIP, WE COULDN'T GO HOME NOW.
WE'D ONLY RISK LEADING THESE MONSTERS BACK THERE IF WE DID.

"FOR MANY LONG MONTHS THEY WANDERED, LIVING OFF THE LAND AND STAYING FAR AWAY FROM THE WAR."
WE'RE LEAVING. THE ADVERSARY'S TROOPS WILL BE HERE SOON.
BUT WHERE CAN YOU **GO** WHERE HIS ARMY CAN'T FOLLOW?

WE'VE HEARD OF A GATEWAY TO A MAGICAL NEW WORLD. A PLACE OF **SANCTUARY.**
TELL YOUR COLONEL HE'S WELCOME TO COME WITH US, BUT DON'T DAWDLE. WE'RE GOING **TODAY.**

"AND DAWDLE THEY DIDN'T. THEY JOINED ONE OF THE MANY FABLE GROUPS MAKING THEIR WAY TO THE NEW WORLD."

AND THAT'S HOW THEY CAME HERE AND FOUNDED SMALLTOWN, UP AT THE FARM?
YEAH, BUT THERE WAS ONE **BIG** PROBLEM THAT BECAME ALMOST IMMEDIATELY APPARENT.

"THE LILLIPUTIAN EXPEDITIONARY FORCE WAS MADE UP ONLY OF **MEN.**"
WHAT ARE YOU GOING TO CALL YOUR NEW HOME?
I THINK WE'VE DECIDED ON **SMALLTOWN.**
I VOTED FOR SMALLVILLE, BUT EVERYONE THOUGHT THAT WAS DUMB.

"THERE WERE NO LILLIPUTIAN WOMEN HERE, SO SMALLTOWN'S FIRST GENERATION THREATENED TO BE ITS LAST."
LILLY AND I WOULD'VE BEEN MARRIED BY NOW.
MY MARY MAY TRIED TO TRAP ME INTO WEDDING HER MANY A TIME. NOW I WISH SHE'D CAUGHT ME.
BUT THERE ARE WOMEN UP IN SMALLTOWN, BIGBY. LOTS OF THEM. I'VE SEEN THEM.
WHO'S TELLING THIS STORY, FLY? YOU OR ME?
SORRY. PLEASE CONTINUE.
"YEARS PASSED WITH NARY A WOMAN IN THE UNHAPPY VILLAGE OF SMALLTOWN-- UNTIL THUMBELINA SHOWED UP, AFTER ESCAPING FROM HER OWN DISTANT HOMELAND."
HI. THE FABLETOWN AUTHORITIES SAID I WOULD BE STAYING HERE, SINCE WE'RE-- UHM--THE SAME SIZE.
A GIRL? A REAL GIRL?
THAT AIN'T NO GIRL, BOY. THAT THAR'S ALL WOMAN.
OH MY!
AND A GORGEOUS ONE AT THAT!

"EVERYONE WAS MISERABLE, NOT THE LEAST OF WHOM OUR PERPETUAL BELLE OF THE BALL.

"THE EVENTUAL SOLUTION TO THEIR DILEMMA CAME FROM AN UNEXPECTED CORNER."
SO MY MOTHER-TO-BE PLANTED THAT KERNEL OF BARLEYCORN IN A FLOWER POT.

"BY THEN, EVERYONE KNEW THUMBELINA'S STORY-- HOW SHE CAME INTO THE WORLD."
AND A TULIP GREW OUT OF IT AND I SPRANG OUT OF THE TULIP BLOSSOM.

"NOW THAT SAME VERY GOOD WITCH-- WHO GAVE THE BARLEYCORN TO THE WOMAN TO GROW HERSELF A DAUGHTER-- HAD ESCAPED THE ADVERSARY AND WAS EVEN THEN LIVING IN FABLETOWN."
OH YES, GAFFER WOLF, I HAD ME A WHOLE JAR FULL OF THEM MAGIC BARLEYCORNS--FULL TO THE TOP.
BUT I DIDN'T ESCAPE WITH THEM. I HAD TOO MUCH TO CARRY AS IT WAS.
I IMAGINE THAT JAR MIGHT STILL BE THERE, BACK IN MY OLD COTTAGE.

"WORD GOT AROUND--WHICH IT WILL--AND PRETTY SOON REACHED BACK UP TO THE FARM, TO THE EARS OF SMALLTOWN'S JOHNNY BULLHORN, A BOLD YOUNG FELLOW FULL OF SPIT AND PEPPER."
I'VE GOT AN IDEA.
WHAT'S THAT, JOHNNY?

I'M GOING BACK TO THE HOMELANDS TO RETRIEVE THE JAR OF MAGIC BARLEYCORNS.
I'VE GOT DETAILED DIRECTIONS TO THE WITCH'S COTTAGE.
COMMANDER ARROW OF THE FARM'S AIR PATROL HAS VOLUNTEERED TO GO WITH ME.
GOOD LUCK, LAD.
KEEP AWAY FROM THE GHOULIES.
AND STAY CLEAR OF LILLIPUT. DON'T RISK LEADING THE GHOULIES THERE EITHER.
MOST OF ALL, BE CAREFUL, JOHNNY.
"SO WITH A FEW MORE WELL-WISHES, AND A CAREFULLY CHASTE KISS FROM THUMBELINA, THE TWO INTREPID FABLES SET OFF ON THEIR GRAND ADVENTURE."
STRAIGHT ON 'TIL MORNING?
SOMETHING LIKE THAT.

"THEY PASSED BACK INTO THE HOMELANDS THROUGH THE OAK HOLLOWS GATE. THIS WAS STILL CLOSE TO FORTY YEARS BEFORE THE ADVERSARY'S WARLOCKS WOULD FIND AND DESTROY IT.

"AND, TRUE TO THEIR WISH, THEY ENJOYED ADVENTURES APLENTY.
"NARROW ESCAPES.

"INCLEMENT WEATHER.

"AND COUNTLESS OTHER HARDSHIPS."
YOU'LL HARDLY MAKE A MOUTHFUL.
COME ANY **CLOSER** AND YOU'LL NIBBLE ON AN INCH OF GOOD MILDENDAN STEEL.

WHAT WAS **THAT** ALL ABOUT?
A GUEST TO SHARE OUR **LUNCH,** BUT HE COULDN'T STAY.
BAH! HE WAS TOO SMALL TO BE RIPE YET ANYWAY.

"AND ALWAYS THEY AVOIDED ANY CONTACT WITH THE ADVERSARY'S OCCUPATION FORCES.

"A FEW MONTHS PASSED, BUT NO ONE WORRIED MUCH. DISTANCES WERE GREATER IN THOSE DAYS."
I WONDER WHERE JOHNNY IS TODAY.
LIVING IN LUXURY IN SOME REMOTE FAIRY CASTLE, I'LL BET, BE-TROTHED TO AN ELF-KING'S HAUNTINGLY BEAUTIFUL DAUGHTER.

"WHEN IT GREW TO SIX MONTHS, WE BEGAN TO FRET A BIT."
HEARD ANYTHING YET, MISS WHITE?
FROM THE FARM? NO, NOTHING YET, MISTER WOLF.

"AND THEN, WHEN A YEAR PASSED, FOLLOWED BY ANOTHER, WE HELD A MEMORIAL SERVICE FOR THE TWO OF THEM. IT WAS UP AT THE FARM, SO I WASN'T ABLE TO ATTEND."
JOHNNY BULLHORN SMALLTOWN HERO
ARROW COMMANDER OF THE AIR PATROL
WE'RE GATHERED HERE ON THIS SOLEMN OCCASION TO REMEMBER TWO OF OUR OWN-- HEROES BOTH.

"WE WERE WRONG THOUGH. THEY WEREN'T DEAD-- BUT IT WOULD BE SOME TIME BEFORE WE LEARNED THAT."
IS THAT IT, ARROW? ARE WE FINALLY HERE?
IT SEEMS SO, JOHNNY.

BUT NO ONE SEEMS TO LIVE HERE ANYMORE.
GOOD.

THEN THERE'S NO ONE TO INTERFERE WITH US WHEN WE GRAB THE TREASURE.
WHAT TREASURE WOULD THAT BE?
THIS PLACE IS EMPTY.

NO TREASURE?
IT'S GONE! ALL GONE!

THEY CLEARED EVERYTHING OUT, LONG AGO!
YOW!
NOW THERE'S AN ODDITY. ONE DOESN'T OFTEN SEE A TALKING MUSTARD POT.

NOT THE JAR, YOU NUMBSKULLS. ME.
OH--UH-- YEAH, I KNEW THAT.

PETE'S MY NAME. MUSTARD POT PETE.
UMM... JOHNNY.
PLEASED T'MEECHA, JOHNNY. SHAKE!

YOU SAID YOU KNEW WHAT HAPPENED TO THE TREASURES STORED HERE?
SPECIFICALLY A JAR OF MAGIC BARLEYCORNS.
OH, SURE.
THE SOLDIERS CAME AND TOOK EVERY-THING YEARS AGO.

TOOK IT ALL TO SOME BIG FORTRESS UP IN THE HIGH HILLS--ALONG WITH EVERY OTHER MAGIC THING IN THIS LAND.
US MERE PEONS AREN'T ALLOWED TO OWN NO MAGICAL STUFF NO MORE.

I'M SURPRISED YOU DON'T ALREADY KNOW THAT.
WE'RE NOT FROM AROUND HERE.
SWIPE!
SWIPE!
SWIPE!

"LONG STORY SHORT -- JOHNNY AND ARROW INVITED PETE TO COME WITH THEM TO GET THE BARLEYCORNS, AND THEN RETURN WITH THEM TO THE FARM."
THERE IT IS, FELLERS! JUST LIKE I TOLDJA!
"PETE WAS RELUCTANT AT FIRST TO LEAVE HIS COMFY MUSTARD POT, BUT FINALLY AGREED WHEN THEY TOLD HIM MANY SUCH SNUG AND HOMEY POTS COULD BE FOUND IN THE NEW WORLD."

WOO HOO! I'M GOING TO PICK OUT SOMETHING TO TAKE BACK WITH ME, TOO!
SHHHHH!
THIS IS SUPPOSED TO BE A COVERT OPERATION.
WHADDAZ THAT MEAN?
BE SNEAKY.

I WONDER WHAT KIND OF FELL BEASTIE THEY HAVE GUARDING THIS PLACE?
THERE'S A GUARD MONSTER?
DIDN'T I MENTION THAT PART?

HOLY CAJOLIES!
AFTER ALL THIS TIME, ARROW! LOOK!
SHUSH! BOTH OF YOU! WHO KNOWS WHAT COULD BE PROWLING AROUND NEARBY?

ARE YOU FELLOWS HERE TO ROB ME?
YEOW!
UH-OH! WE'RE DOOMED NOW!

NO! HONEST! WE JUST CAME TO SAY HELLO.
THESE ARE YOUR TREASURES, MISTER BEAR?
ONLY IN THE SENSE THAT I WAS PLACED HERE, BY THE EMPIRE'S LOCAL GOVERNOR, TO GUARD THEM.

WHAT DID YOU HOPE TO FIND HERE?
A JAR OF MAGIC BARLEYCORNS.
OH, THOSE. YOU'LL FIND THEM ON THE THIRD SHELF, OVER THERE.
YOU'RE GOING TO LET US TAKE THEM?

YOU'RE NOT GOING TO EAT US?
I'D NEVER EAT YOU. I'M ACCUS-TOMED TO BETTER CUISINE THAN YOU'D PROVIDE.

ACTUALLY, I'M A POWERFUL SORCERER-KING--WELL, AN EX-KING NOW. I'M SUPPOSED TO TURN INTRUDERS INTO FROGS, OR PORCELAIN STATUES, OR--
I DON'T WANT TO BE NO FROG!
FROGS EAT BUGS!

"AFTER A SURPRISINGLY PLEASANT AFTERNOON'S CONVERSATION, THEY LOCATED THE BARLEYCORN JAR."
HOW ARE WE GOING TO CARRY THIS ALL THE WAY BACK TO OUR WORLD?
GOOD QUESTION.
I THOUGHT I WOULD CARRY IT-- AND THE THREE OF YOU AS WELL.

YOU'RE COMING WITH US?
IF COMMANDER ARROW COULD BE PERSUADED TO LEND ME HIS WINGS FOR A FEW DAYS.

I HAD NO STRONG DESIRE TO SERVE THE INVADERS, BUT AT LEAST IN THIS JOB THEY LEAVE ME ALONE FOR THE MOST PART.
AND, UNTIL NOW, I HAD NOWHERE ELSE TO GO. I THOUGHT THEY'D ALREADY CONQUERED EVERY LAND.

THIS SHOULDN'T HURT TOO MUCH, COMMANDER ARROW.
OH MY.

"BY NOW, YOU'VE FIGURED OUT THE REST OF THIS TALE.
"JOHNNY AND ARROW FLEW HOME, BRINGING THEIR NEW FRIENDS WITH THEM.

"THEY WERE WARMLY GREETED ON THEIR RETURN."
WELCOME HOME, JOHNNY!
MUSTARD POT PETE'S THE NAME! PLEASED T'MEECHA!

"AND A GREAT BIG CROP OF BARLEYCORN GIRLS WERE GROWN THAT VERY SPRING."

"FIVE COUPLES WERE UNITED IN THAT FIRST OF MANY WEDDINGS TO COME.
"THE MAGIC BEAR GAVE ARROW HIS WINGS BACK AND LIVED ON THE FARM FOR A FEW CENTURIES, BEFORE GETTING A HANKERING TO LIVE DOWN IN THE CITY.
"HE TRANSFORMED HIMSELF INTO MISTER GRANDOURS, WHO LIVES UP ON THE NINTH FLOOR.
"PETE FOUND HIMSELF ANOTHER COZY, DISCARDED MUSTARD POT TO MOVE INTO.
"AND YOUNG JOHNNY BULLHORN WAS KNOWN FROM THAT DAY FORWARD AS JOHN BARLEYCORN.
"HE HAD MANY OTHER ADVENTURES, WHICH ARE TALES FOR ANOTHER TIME."

AFTER THAT FIRST CROP, THERE WERE MORE THAN ENOUGH WOMEN IN SMALLTOWN TO CREATE MORE BOYS AND GIRLS THE OLD-FASHIONED WAY.
SO THE JAR OF REMAINING BARLEYCORNS WAS MOVED DOWN HERE, TO BE STORED SAFELY WITH THE REST OF OUR MAGIC THINGS.
BUT BOYS WILL BE BOYS, AND IT QUICKLY BECAME A SMALLTOWN TRADITION FOR EVERY YOUNG MAN TO SNEAK DOWN HERE AND TRY, AT LEAST ONCE, TO WIN HIMSELF A BARLEYCORN BRIDE, BEFORE GOING HOME TO MARRY THE GIRL NEXT DOOR.
ROBBERY
BURGLARY
GRAND THEFT
LARCENY
PLAGIARISM
WHY?
COPY

MANY REASONS, I GUESS. A DESIRE TO WIN STATUS IN THE COMMUNITY BY IMITATING WHAT JOHN BARLEYCORN DID.
AND THE BARLEYCORNS ARE REPUTED TO BE FAR LOVELIER THAN ANY NORMAL GIRL--THEIR SIZE OR OURS.
OKAY, FLY, YOU'VE HAD YOUR STORY. WE BOTH HAVE THINGS TO DO.

THANKS, SHERIFF. YOU KNOW, YOU'RE NOT NEARLY AS MEAN AS EVERYONE SAYS YOU... UH--I'LL GET BACK TO WORK NOW.
THE END.